From

the

Darkness

One Woman's Rise
to Nobility

The Autobiography

of

Connie Morris

Huntington House Publishers

Huntington House Publishers
P.O. Box 53788
Lafayette, Louisiana 70505

PRINTED IN THE UNITED STATES OF AMERICA.

Library of Congress Card Catalog Number 2001097469
ISBN 1-56384-194-0

Preface

A chicken farm in the Appalachian Mountains sounds hick, doesn't it? You see, hicks or hillbillies are usually happy with themselves, satisfied to be uneducated, inbred, and uncouth; we were none of these, and neither were we happy.

My parents owned and operated a prosperous poultry farm, boasting over 70,000 laying hens, sometimes employing over twenty men and women to gather, cultivate, pack, and deliver eggs. The delivery route covered three states, servicing large national grocery chains, as well as "Mom and Pop" country stores. The farm was perched high atop a hill which was covered with majestic trees and profuse undergrowth. Climbing the driveway was like traveling through a tunnel. Trees towered above, hiding the sky before suddenly opening to a picturesque estate. Our home was painted pale yellow with a shaded veranda lined in cut stone and supported with wrought iron posts, the kind with iron ivy winding perfectly to its summit. A set of expensive wrought iron furniture charmed guests with its quaint, inviting appearance, although it was hard and uncomfortable. Rarely did anyone sit there. It was a façade, like so many other things in our family. Resting in soothing stillness was not an option.

As a child, I loved my parents. I especially cherished my mother. Through the years of disappointments and anguish, I have come to love them more. This is the story of how that happened. The ugliness contained within may be shocking (possibly *too* graphic for certain readers), but I feel it necessary in order to take you to where the abused is crouched.

By way of disclaimer, my humble personal opinion on abuse will emerge. Biblical truths are presented as facts, and absolutely every account is told in the purest of truth. Although, perhaps, as the people who wear them, some names have been masked. The purpose of this book is to simply share a story that many may want to hear.

Jesus Christ was and continues to be my answer to sanity and success, and I'm convinced He is your only hope as well. This autobiography is directed toward a wide range of readers and is intended for use in secular settings as well as on the church scene. For that reason, I will attempt to steer clear of "preaching" and leave much of the interpretation to you or the Holy Spirit, whomever you are depending on at this point in the game. It comes to you with hope and prayer that somehow it will enrich or encourage you or someone you love dearly.

Chapter One

The chickens cackled an orchestral backdrop to my early childhood. I never attended to the noise or stench. Visitors squealed as they held their noses and complained that they couldn't sleep from all the racket. My parents let neither of these factors hinder them. They both worked long, hard hours, and were very successful at what they did. My father, reportedly of Indian heritage, was tall with dark hair and deep, drowning, crystal eyes. Mom was petite and full-figured, with a beautiful face that made you want to linger with her a little longer. Because of that fact, and despite the ongoing clamor of the futuristic machinery, I would often fall asleep in the "egg room" just to be close to her during late nights at work. Her job was to lift heavy cases of freshly-gathered, dirty eggs onto a table, then gently place the eggs on rollers that were underlain with lights. As the eggs rolled over the lights, she was to inspect for blood spots or tiny cracks in the delicate shells. I dare say my dear Mother has handled, viewed, and culled trillions of eggs in her lifetime, and she did so stoically.

Dad was usually away from the farm on business trips. I remember very few dinners with him. Actually, I remember only one . . . we had gravy that night, with fresh, green onions chopped up in it. Somehow Mom managed to raise a garden with plenty of fresh vegetables for the summer. We usually did manage to have breakfast together as a family. Dad would look at his watch, sometime before I had the sleep rubbed out of my eyes, and gasp, "Jeepers creepers, I've got to get to work!" And there went my beloved Daddy, out to make a living for us. Ironically, he was allergic to feathers and couldn't eat eggs or chicken. Mom, as I remember, ran the everyday details of the operation. She had an office desk in her bedroom and would get up every morning around 5:00 A.M. to do the bookkeeping. That office would later prove to be in a hazardous location.

I saw my parents kiss twice; both were quick "thank you" pecks. The first time was a rare playful moment at our round, oak kitchen table, which sat in front of a huge picture window that peeked over the hill behind our lovely home. The second and last time was close to their divorce. Dad had returned from a business trip bearing the usual gifts for us all. He brought Mom a fur collar. She received it graciously, as she forced herself to smile and dutifully thank him with a smooch on the cheek.

I was the youngest of three siblings. Cindy was the oldest. I was never close to her as a child. She always disliked me, and recounted years later that she strongly resented me. Billy was the middle child and my playmate. We had great fun running the hills and playing in the woods. We were best friends and I stuck to him like glue. Since our parents worked endless, lonely hours and my sister avoided me, he was all I had until I started school. Billy was also Dad's favorite offspring, and he often gained affection from Dad that we girls never got. If I played my cards right (and I usually did), I might enjoy some of the attention that was directed toward my brother but was broad enough to spread to his shadow of a sister. Billy didn't mind; he watched out for me and made sure I ate when there wasn't a meal on the table. The three of us weren't raised up; we were jerked up. And no matter what, we stuck together.

I had a dog named Chico, and she was the instrument through which I would witness God's first *known-to-me* miracle. Chico was impregnated by one of the many stray mutts that roam the hills of Kentucky. Dad said I could keep only one of the pups. The rest would go in a sack with a rock and be thrown to the bottom of the pond. So I prayed that Chico would have only *one* pup. I prayed hard and told my family and some of the work hands of my expectations. I made Chico a cozy bed in the garage, right beside the door that immediately entered our sweet smelling kitchen. From there I kept a close watch on her.

Me as a toddler in the early 60s, the youngest of three.

Chico was getting big, and Mom was beginning to prepare me for the ensuing, unwanted, large litter that was about to arrive. One night a pack of stray dogs got in the garage and were fighting with Chico. There were ten to fifteen wild beasts right beside our garage door, snarling and attacking my pet. I heard the ruckus and climbed out of bed. I tried to break up the fight by repeatedly opening and slamming the garage door and screaming at the top of my lungs. It didn't do a lot to hinder the vicious rumble taking place a few feet away from me, but it did awaken the entire family. Dad jumped out of bed, grabbed his gun, loaded it quickly, and went out shooting. The sun was coming up just as the shots stopped ringing out. The family had stayed inside, and Mom was trying to calm me. My brother and sister were irritated with me. Dad walked in the door with little to say. I looked out onto the beautifully landscaped lawn and saw dead dogs scattered about the yard. He put away his rifle and went back out to discard the carcasses. At that moment, he became my hero. No little girl was more proud of, or possessed more love for, her Daddy than I. A few weeks later, Chico gave birth to *one,* strapping, little pup—an event that was heralded by many (even unbelievers) as a merciful gift from God Himself to a child whose life was rapidly disintegrating into a world where puppies and prayer didn't matter.

Mom told me once that all their marital problems started when I was born, not *because* I was born (I think). I believe she was trying to give me a time frame of events, while attempting to explain to a 6-year-old why her home-life was in turmoil. Mom and Dad argued continuously, and many times their altercations turned into fist fights or hurling objects through the air toward each other. I remember seeing Dad hovering over Mom beating her with his fist, and Mom doubled up below him on the couch screaming and trying to shelter herself from the blows. Mom *did* however manage to return a few of her own punches. One time she threw an iron skillet at Dad, and another time she took a picture off the wall and slung it at him. It hit his leg and glass shattered across the floor. Once, during a loud argument, I jumped between them and held out my arms like a traffic officer with a whistle clenched in his puckered lips and a cord dangling from around his neck. I cried and begged them to stop fighting. It didn't help matters at all. My acknowledgment of their shortcomings only infuriated each of them and heightened the intensity of the fight. I was verbally removed from the room, and I never tried that trick again.

Another horrendous fight took place one day when a business associate was visiting our farm. It wasn't unusual for a lot of people to travel in and out of our quarter-mile, private driveway. We sold eggs directly from the factory, and many local people came there to purchase them fresh. Our home was a few hundred yards from the chicken houses and egg room, which made it convenient for people to knock on our door at any time for a variety of reasons. One particular day, a man (who was the major supplier for the packaging cartons we used) stopped by our house. Since Mom needed to go over some business with him, she led him to her bedroom/office (yikes!) and started pulling out books and records. He sat down beside her desk and they completed the task at hand. As they were exiting the bedroom, Dad showed up and his outrageous jealousy exploded. He pounded the bewildered associate with his fists as he slung him across the room a few feet at a time. With each stumbling blow the man groped his way toward the door, while Dad spewed profanities and threats at him. I don't remember what happened next, except it was a controversial and expensive chore to find a new supplier for egg cartons.

Dad was, and still is, a Baptist minister. He pastors a church a few miles down the road. It's actually called a Primitive Baptist Church . . . that's what the sign really says outside. Some people call them "hard-shell" Baptist. During services, men and women sit on opposite sides of the sanctuary. They don't believe in an "altar" (it must be called a platform), they don't allow music, and they practice line singing. (This is a peculiar form of art that is dying out, but is quite intriguing and has the essence of a Gregorian Chant.) The pastor sings a line of the song, and the congregation drones out the words after him in repetition, while keeping to an ever-slight fluctuation in melody. I suppose it was a tradition that began before printed songbooks were common. Instead of "Revivals," they have "Associations." All the local Primitive Baptist churches take turns hosting the great gatherings. Back then, people would come in campers and stay for days. The preachers (any male would do) lined up on the pew behind the podium facing frontward and "tag preached." When one red-faced, sweaty, preacher was out of breath from screaming about the love of God, he would shake hands with another preacher, pulling him up to take over and continue the impudent, so-called sermon. At noon, a magnificent feast was spread across makeshift tables outside under the trees. The women put on a display of their favorite home-cooked recipes while the men rested in the shade and waited to be called upon to pass the blessing. After lunch, the women cleaned and put away the food while the others returned indoors to resume the preaching. Women were not allowed to speak during church but were expected to shout and cry. Often a song would break out and everyone would walk around shaking hands, kissing on the cheek, and hugging. The kids were usually outside playing in the creek that trickled politely behind the church. We would check in when we heard them singing, perhaps (we hoped) it was the last song. Today the church is usually empty, with only a few members and less than ten people showing up for their monthly gatherings.

Mom didn't always attend church with Dad. The style of worship was very different from her Pilgrim Holiness/Wesleyan upbringing. And of course, I'm sure the hypocrisy on Dad's part was more than she could stomach. Every Sunday morning, a mysteriously initiated fight arose between Mom and Dad as to whom would have us kids in tow for church. Dad's church didn't meet on Sunday evening, but Mom's church did, and she was faithfully there every week. Dad spitefully used Walt Disney (the hit Sunday evening program) as leverage to convince us to stay home with him instead of accompanying Mom to church. We had a new Zenith console, color television which was a luxurious enchantment to small children of the sixties. That ploy worked most times on Billy and Cindy, but I felt sorry for Mom and would accompany her to "her" church. It was called Garvin Ridge Wesleyan Church. They had a longtime pastor named Brother Walter Duncan, and what a man he was! He was a kind, gentle man that could convict a rock of sin. He spoke of the love of Jesus while crossing the street with a stranger or friend. He would kick up his heels and shout praises to God as fervently as he described the atrocities of Hell. There was a sweet spirit in that church, and I liked it. It was like a warm blanket during a frigid snowstorm. I eventually snubbed that warm, sweet, comfort, yet pursued it in numerous forms, only to spend many years becoming more and more wretched, cold, and deeply injured.

Chapter Two

My parents tried a variety of arrangements in order to maintain a working relationship and keep the family together. For a brief period of time, Dad set up a bed in the basement and tried to act like it was normal to be sleeping with the mice and spiders. I started to learn what the word "divorce" meant and began to pray it wouldn't happen to my parents. It was the 1960s; Americans witnessed men walking on the moon and the murder of a beloved president, but people didn't speak of abuse, nor were women permitted to disparage their husbands or hope for marital help from outsiders, including family.

Dad was a master at masking the reality of his troubled marriage, perhaps multiplying Mom's disgust.

Husbands and wives weren't readily divorcing, and I never truly believed it would happen to *my* parents.

I started school at age six, with a wonderful Christian teacher. Mrs. Janet Maddix remains an inspiration to me today. She has written several books of poetry and has visited me thirty years later at my ranch home, far away from the hills of Kentucky. During my first-grade year in school, I experienced a loss of hearing in my left ear. While sitting in class, at a half-moon-reading table, I struggled to hear the other children read aloud the basil stories of Jan and her dog, Tip. Mrs. Maddix finally insisted my parents have me checked by a specialist. I remember visiting several doctors and undergoing tests. There was a slight scare that I may be going deaf, I hoped it would be serious enough to end my parents' fighting and keep things together. My shallow plan was rattled when impacted earwax was easily removed, and my perfect hearing was restored.

However, a little time later, exciting, new hope sprang up when Mom became pregnant with her fifth child (their first child was carried to full term but died during birth). It seemed I was told of the baby, and then . . . there Mom was . . . with a big belly and tired feet. Despite her condition and a history of complicated pregnancies, she continued to work long hours on the farm.

My paternal grandparents owned a crowded, little country store which I loved visiting. I didn't like spending the night at their house though, after my cousin Reggie, a grown teenager, caressed me in his bed in a way that made my stomach sick. Unexpectedly one day, Dad picked up Cindy, Billy, and I after school and took us to Mamaw and Papaw Littleton's grocery store. It was time to go to the hospital and have the baby, and we were to stay at their home for the night. I was excited, but somehow I knew something was wrong.

I don't remember anything of being told the baby was stillborn. I only recall the nausea that I experienced at the funeral and would suffer with for years to come. Mom was still hospitalized during the funeral, so it was up to Dad to play the trooper. Tiers of flowers with clashing scents dutifully stood guard throughout the ceremony. My stair-step siblings and I sat on the front unpadded pew of Dad's uncarpeted church and listened to sad, monotonous songs being droned out, unaccompanied by music. My soul felt numb. I was 8-years-old and still played with dolls. But when I saw my baby sister, a perfect doll, lying lifeless, with full, black locks of hair, in a pink, velvet-lined and tufted, two-foot casket, my make-believe world faded like the heavy fog that lingers in the hollow until early noon. Reality was coming home at a dangerous speed to me as a little girl in the Appalachian Mountains . . . as it does to so many little children.

Mom had lost her first and last child, Tony Lou and Cora Lou respectively, and a part of her was carried away and buried with them. It seemed to take her many months to regain her strength. As her joy and hope waned, so did the family unit and her marriage. She became bitter, angry, and just plain tired. I badly wanted her to feel better and tried to help any way I could. Cindy became rebellious and fought vehemently with Mom. Billy remained quiet and broken up inside.

School days passed by with bittersweet memories. Our school was an old building with high ceilings and wooden floors. Tall, inefficient windows were propped open with a book in the summer heat, allowing flies to swarm through the unscreened openings. The school was called Upper Tygart Elementary, distinguishing its location on the upper bank of Tygart Creek. The teachers were basically good people, nice country folks that attended church and had genuine concern for others. I was a cute little kid, always too curious for my own good, but energetic, fun loving, and likeable. Our school mascot was the Tigers, and I began a long, unhealthy interest in cheerleading. Mr. Calhoun was our principal, and he had taken a special interest in my future. As in most small school districts, the faculty and staff held several positions as club sponsors, etc. Thus Mr. Calhoun became my 4-H speech leader. Five of us gathered in his small office to recite our speeches daily. My speech was about the virtues of 4-H, and it included a joke about a mouse. I knew the speech well and grew tired of rehearsing it. Refusing to regurgitate the speech "one more time" evoked a lecture from Mr. Calhoun on how talented I was and how I had to get rid of my stubborn, perhaps cocky confidence. I disagreed. I made it all the way to state competition with that speech!

Mom sewed me a pair of elephant-ear pants and attached a 4-H emblem to a matching white tank top. The family loaded up for a venture to the big city. I was to present my speech at the University of Kentucky in Lexington, before noon. I was underdressed and extremely nervous, but I delivered the speech to my satisfaction. Several hundred participants gathered in a comfortable and fairly elaborate auditorium for the awards ceremony. The emcee requested the parents of the Grand Champion to please accompany their child to the stage when the winner was announced. Mom whispered, "I hope you don't win because I don't want to go up there!" It was a jest, but it hit hard, and I resented it. My family sat impatiently awaiting my name to be called. Excitement mounted as the emcee eliminated many participants and finally hesitated as he announced the reserve and Grand Champion. My heart pounded. I wanted to win first place but I didn't want Mom to be put through any more grief. She had been through so much. "Okay, Lord," I prayed breathlessly, "I'll take second place." Just then my name was called over the microphone; and I went forward, alone, to accept my Reserve Grand Champion red ribbon and medal.

Late one summer night (I think it was 1972) Mom and Dad called us kids to the living room for a talk. The television was unusually void. The 60s room had newly-purchased, lined, heavy drapes with large, orange flowers splattered across a pale, sick-green background. Between the drapes hung perfectly-pleated, light-orange, sheer curtains. The windows were open at the bottom, and the thin sheer curtains gently billowed in the humid, Kentucky breeze. Both our parents sat on the sectional couch that nearly stretched the length of two walls. They proceeded gently and decisively as they announced they had agreed to divorce. Cindy was busying herself during the dreaded scene with a pot of water, which she hurled across the room at the first moment of silence. Billy and I cried in the corner . . . and then we were told to go to bed.

With anger and anguish, Cindy looks away. Billy boldly remains hopeful and, for the moment, I'm unsure of the unfolding drama.

I'm not sure how my parents planned for the separation to come about, or for that matter, if they planned the following months at all! There were a lot of things to work out, as in most divorces, and this marriage was not going to go down smoothly. I often wonder where my parents held God during this time. I'm sure they were both praying desperately for God's guidance and peace. Mom would kneel each night in the dark living room and pray until she sobbed quietly. Sometimes I would try to comfort her, but it was important to not get caught by Dad (I'm not sure why). Most obviously they were concerned for us kids, and rightfully so. Still it seemed the majority of their energies were focused on what to do next, sometimes moment to moment.

Mom's asylum was clutched nearby in the grip of an evil doer . . . one of our male employees. Many years later, she would pay a dear price for his support during her pending deliverance from an abusive husband and miserable marriage. Dad seemed oblivious to the turmoil. He was not nurturing nor tended to our needs as children. He felt his main responsibility was to work long, hard hours and preach on Sunday. I remember few playful encounters with Dad. I recall holding his hand only once while skipping along with him as he darted about his work on the farm, rather inconvenienced, but nonetheless forcing himself to provide a rare moment of attention for his pre-schooler. Standing below his waist, I friskily suspended my weight from his long, muscular arm and giggled in hope of a romp with my daddy. Instead he scolded me loudly as he yanked his hand from my tiny grasp, nearly landing me on my backside. Family vacations were spent with Dad at the driver's wheel and everybody trying not to evoke an argument. Now he was losing his family, and I sensed he was sad, but yet almost elated to be ridding himself of Mom's incessant anger. Tragically, he would spend the rest of his life dysfunctionally groping for more than he had.

Dad purchased a small, low-grade, two-bedroom, single-wide mobile home. He parked it beside the recently-constructed egg-processing plant, situated conveniently along side the main highway that traversed the region. That was to be his home, and Mom and the kids were to remain in the house. A noble plan, but one that hardly got off the ground.

We were considered a wealthy family. It was very important to Dad to be successful in the business realm. His materialism surmounted his income and resulted in great debt. Several miles away, the interstate system was nearing completion, and posed a threat to Dad's business as the traffic passing through continued to decline. Mom continued the bookkeeping, as well as helping in the factory and managing the now superficially prosperous enterprise. The new plant was built just a short while before Mom and Dad decided to divorce. It likely was fuel to an already volatile relationship.

Everyone was proud of the new factory, as it boldly announced its presence in a small-time, rural community. The back of the structure housed the loading docks and faced a rippling creek that was hidden from view by mossy trees and ferns. There was a huge, refrigerated room between the docks and packaging room. Two offices were found in the front of the building, along with a kitchen and restrooms for the employees. The front office was suppose to be the receptionist/

secretary's, but Mom usually chose to do her work at home. She did, however, help decorate it with matching green, leather furniture. A large picture of wild horses hung handsomely next to demographic maps and framed magazine articles proclaiming Dad's success. The arrangement seemed to be working fairly well. Then plans were made to host a community dance for our school friends and neighbors in our beautiful, new building.

Cindy, Billy, and I invited everyone we knew, even the hired hands. Violet Hamm, who had been working for us for many years and loved us dearly, would come and help chaperone. The floors were swept and the stereo was set up days in advance. On the evening of the dance, my brother, sister, and I were so excited that we decided to walk a mile and a half from our house to the plant, in order to arrive early. Our parents were never ones to make arrangements with us, as to where we were, or where *they* were, or when we were suppose to be somewhere. So showing up unplanned didn't seem to be a problem. We walked in the front entrance, hot and thirsty from the long walk. It was a sultry, humid day and the large, roll-up doors were open on each end of the building to allow air to circulate through the unairconditioned, massive structure.

It seemed that time stopped ticking when our eyes fell upon the piteous jumble of a once attractive reception room. Maps were torn in half on the wall, leaving two ripped sides taped to the corrugated, metal siding. A large, indoor, potted houseplant that stood on a stand in the corner had been overturned and dirt was strewn across the commercial-grade, tightly woven, blue-green carpet. Our mouths hung open in silence as we precariously tiptoed through the papers and items on the floor to get past the mess. We looked all through the building and yelled for Mom and Dad, but there seemed to be no one around. We retreated to the makeshift dancehall and decided to await our friends. Anxiety replaced fear as the appointed time for the dance to begin drew closer. Finally Violet arrived right on time to help with refreshments. She had no idea as to the whereabouts of our parents, but we were all confident that there was a reasonable explanation for the circumstances, and in my mind, the ensuing party took precedence over any crisis that could possibly arise. Mom showed up shortly after Violet and briefly explained that she and Dad had gotten into a fight, and it resulted in the torn-up office. That wasn't a big surprise to us, and we took it in stride. But more importantly, it was time for the dance to begin, and yet no guests had arrived. We turned on the music and dimmed the lights to set the mood, but still no guests. Finally a neighbor friend came over in response to our obligatory invitation. He and his family were nice as far as neighbors go, but neither our parents nor we were ever close friends. None the less, we were thrilled to see him! Awkward moments passed as we waited for more "friends" to join us. Locusts began to hum in the trees that covered the surrounding hills.

Dusk was setting when suddenly Dad recklessly appeared in our brand new, green, Chevy Impala. He was literally swerving from ditch line to ditch line before he managed to slide into the white, graveled parking lot. The tires threw tiny rocks against the new, light green, aluminum siding before the car spun in a half circle and landed daringly in front of the opened ten-foot doors to our nonexistent party. Dad emerged from the driver's seat, carrying a new shoebox and staggering uncontrollably. I had never seen a drunk person, but I was sure he was soused, and there was about to be a big fight! He stumbled up to Billy and proudly handed him a new pair of tennis shoes. The shoestrings were spilling over the outer edge of the box as Billy reached out for the shoes. He was speechless and struggling to hold back tears of confusion and sorrow. Dad began to mumble at Cindy and me, something about "I love you too, but your Mom . . ." Mom picked up the pace and started shouting at Dad. Billy stole center stage when he cursed Dad and threw the shoes in his direction. The opened box slid across the concrete and came to a stop at Dad's steel-toed work boots. Then Billy took off outside and headed for the woods. By now it was completely dark, and I knew it wasn't a good thing for Billy to be out there alone.

Dad began to cry helplessly and stumbled back to the car. He drove away a little more sobered, but equally as numbing to me as his arrival. Our neighbor friend left without much of a farewell. Mom thanked him for coming. Violet tried to comfort each of us but was obviously relieved to be leaving. Mom, Cindy, and I were left standing in the middle of a large empty room surrounded by the buzzing of overhead, florescent lights and thousands of astonished night bugs that played audience to the drama. I wished I could be like them, taking sanctuary atop a tall Oak or under a carpet of soft, green moss. It must have been God's mercy that kept our friends away that night, although we were each greatly disappointed. I believe our friends and their parents must have sensed the jeopardy that hovered repulsively over our family, and they simply stayed away. Mom went looking for Billy, while Cindy and I attempted to clean the office. She returned without him, so all we could do was hope he would find his way safely through the woods back to the house.

It was near midnight when we turned out all the lights and started out the door to go home. Erroneous timing placed us in the parking lot as Dad returned, this time violently enraged and broadcasting his intent to kill our mother and demanding we stay out of his way! Mom and Dad began to wrestle, with Mom screaming and Dad spluttering obscenities. Despite his inebriated state, Dad was succeeding at doing some serious damage beneath his ferocious blows. Somehow Cindy managed to get Mom and me back inside behind locked doors. Cindy ran to the kitchen and retrieved a butcher knife from a drawer in the employee lunchroom. She grabbed me and ordered me to get behind the heavy, locked steel door and stay down. Dad was pounding at the door, now cursing Cindy as well as Mom, and threatening to unlock the door if somebody didn't open it. Terror gripped me as I realized he did, of course, have the necessary key dangling from his expandable key chain affixed to his belt. I joined in the screaming, and it was just the needed antidote to diffuse the attack. Dad must have begun to realize what he was doing. His voice calmed, and he tried to reassure us he would never hurt us. Mom, Cindy, and I were huddled behind the door, in stark blackness, staring through stinging tears at the glowing, silver doorknob. We listened intently for a key to slide into the lock and the knob to turn, commencing a scene too horrible to imagine. Moments later we heard the side entrance door shut and Dad driving away. It was over as quickly as it began.

I don't remember how or when we found Billy, but the next thing I recall is all of us heading to our maternal grandmother's house to stay the night . . . what was left of it. She was elderly and couldn't be bothered with a lot of disturbance. So we compliantly found a spot in her tiny house to rest our heads and waited for the sun to rise. At daybreak Mom suggested Billy and I walk down the creek bank to look at an old house that belonged to Mom's sister and brother-in-law and had been vacant for years. "Perhaps we could move into it," she weakly suggested. Cindy was considered mature enough to stay in the room while Mom explained to her mother why we had fled there in the early morning hours.

Billy and I found the abandoned shack. We peered through the filthy, broken windows and beheld the shelter that could soon replace our beautiful modern home on the hill. Fortunately, that idea was soon discarded. It was decided that Mom, Cindy, and I would take the recently purchased, mobile home to a rented lot in the nearest town, Olive Hill, and Dad and Billy would stay in the house on the hill.

Splitting up the siblings was a dreadful mistake, but the whole situation was so misfortunate that I think we each lost interest in caring. Each of us kids began to shut down emotionally, coping with the arrangements in our own afflicted way. Billy chose to stay with Dad, but Dad hardly left room for a real choice to be made by anyone, especially Mom. His favoritism for Billy and deadly threats against losing custody of him were easily effective against Mom's feeble attempts and hopes to keep the children together. I think Billy grew to resent Mom for "allowing" him to be pulled from Cindy and me. As a little boy, he felt abandoned by his mother, a misconception endowed by our manipulative father.

Chapter Three

Mom obtained a job at one of several sewing factories in town. She was "on production," which meant the more garments she constructed, the more she was paid. So she worked hard in sweatshop-type conditions. Dad was either unable or unwilling to provide much by way of financial support. I think it was a little of both.

Cindy took the center, small bedroom, and Mom and I were to share the back bedroom. I didn't like sleeping with Mom, because it was stifling and uncomfortable. I was accustomed to my own bed in my perfectly decorated, fit-for-a-princess bedroom. So the couch became my bed. It was shabbily constructed with more cardboard than wood and sparsely placed, unforgiving springs. The upholstery was green-and-yellow plaid, with a rough texture and low thread count. Violet Hamm gave me a used diary, which I began to write in regularly. I kept it hidden under the bathroom sink, and nightly I entered my heartaches and sins without discretion.

*   *   *   *   *

The Fourth of July in Olive Hill, Kentucky, is celebration time. Tom T. Hall, a country music star known as The Storyteller, was reared in our neck of the woods and was, therefore, traditionally invited to put on an annual concert for the town. A parade of red, white, and blue everything marched down the hill in front of the local drive-in and continued to the other end of main street . . . a monumental two miles! People came out of the woodwork and squeezed in for the activities. A shear cliff nudged one side of Main Street, and the opposite side was lined with mostly-vacant, two-story, brick buildings. This once booming town was now the loser in competition with a neighboring college town and a freeway that didn't come quite close enough to boost economy.

Billy got a new 650 Honda motorcycle for his birthday (one of Dad's bribes for his devotion). A male friend and I asked to borrow it to ride in the parade. Billy grudgingly obliged. The parade was fun, and we should have ended the good time there, but my sense of adventure took over. We headed out of town, cruising the back roads and enjoying the day. We decided to ride through the nearby state park. It was a magnificent drive that took a lot of turns under splendid, sprawling trees of many sorts. I was enjoying the tranquility when I felt the bike skid against the momentum of a sharp curve. I looked down and saw that we were on the left of the double, yellow line by a good twelve inches. The tires squealed as they slid through the curve and left a smoking, black skid mark. I felt heroic when it seemed we were going to clear the curve without incident. The rush was exuberating, a dare against death that I wanted to repeat. Just then a car met us head on. The motorcycle completed its sideways skid and crashed with great force against the front grill of the oncoming vehicle. My body took flight and sailed through the upper limbs of a huge tree, nearly fifty feet into the air. I landed over the hill in a cornfield with a deafening, empty thud. My breath was knocked out, and I gasped with laborious effort to achieve an intake of air. People were rushing to my side. My friend had hurt his leg but was able to walk and had climbed down the hill to where I lay. He knelt over me with an expression that frightened me. I slowly regained shallow but sufficient breathing and was relieved when bystanders removed my helmet. The chinstrap had unsnapped, but fortunately the helmet remained in place during the crash. After close examination, it was discovered the helmet had cracked down the middle upon impact. An ambulance arrived, and imminent damage to my neck and spine lurked over the huddle as I was carefully loaded onto a board that would hopefully protect my body until I arrived at the hospital. EMT's struggled to get me up the steep embankment and were loading me into the ambulance when I lifted my eyes and rasped, "Tom T. Hall!" He was on his way to the concert when we met abruptly in the curve and was watching the scene unfold with obvious concern. I was later released from the hospital with no serious or permanent injury.

*   *   *   *   *

My seventh grade school year was soon to begin, and I would be attending a new school. I was proud of Cindy as she marched me into the school's principal's office for enrollment. She knew the school operated on a tracking system, something of which I knew nothing about. Track One was the elite, attractive, A+ students; Track Two was for the B-C, middle income, plain looking, and moderately dressed students. Track Three was special education. She boldly presented my previous year's grade card and insisted I could *and should* be placed in Track One. She quickly briefed me on the conditions before entering the office. I was told, if asked, to state that school was easy for me, and I could intelligently interact with students in Track One. "Don't act or *say* anything stupid!" she instructed, "Let me do the talking." So I did, and we exited the school successful. I began to trust Cindy and need her near me in a new way. We had never been close sisters. Until that summer, we had fought with endless and vicious malice. When school began, Billy was in the eighth grade and still at Upper Tygart, I was in Olive Hill just eight miles away, and Cindy was a senior at the only centrally-located high school, also in Olive Hill.

Autumn in Kentucky is gorgeous. Thousands of trees don new apparel in shades unmixable and uncaptured on most artists' palettes. It's a beautiful time that unfortunately doesn't last long. Usually a heavy rain or early frost will cause the multitude of colored leaves to fall too quickly to the ground. As a child I loved traipsing through the dense woods, listening to the sound of the dusty, crisp, dried leaves crunching under my small feet. Sometimes my brother and I would scrape up a huge pile of the colorful foliage and belly dive right into the middle of the mound. However, this autumn of 1973 would provide the backdrop for the disgraceful, near annihilation of my innocence. The leaves would fall, and the trees would become completely bare, just as my spirit would become. I would lack luster and be without color. My skin would become pale, and blackness would encircle my once sparkling, gleeful green eyes. The trees appeared, just as I did, to be dying.

Hollow hearts and piercing pain impregnates each of us as we battle through the first year of "our" divorce.

I made friends with Tamera Gossett, a girl who lived down the street. Her mother was also divorced, and we shared a keen passion for gymnastics and cheerleading. When tryouts were held that fall, we were both easily selected. It was exciting to become popular in an already competitive class. Boys began to pay intense attention to me. Tamera had long lost her virginity and prudence, (by her choice and with eager consent) and was thus prime prey for the uncontrolled mongers that were far too common in the sixties and seventies. Our friendship and my loneliness set the stage for a trail of boyfriends to be called mine. Sometimes I would change the "boy I liked" twice in one day. I got kissed for the first time in the back row of the movie house while pretentiously watching John Wayne in *True Grit*.

I "went steady" with a new boy every few weeks. My friends and I naively described sexual behavior as "playing baseball." We fondled and petted each other like uncouth hounds, while remaining childishly on first base. Mom was unaware of my behavior. She was consumed with her own anxieties *and* boyfriend.

Don Clark was a previous employee of Pine Grove Poultry Farm, the title of my parents' business. He had made advances toward Mom while working with her and was at the plant the day of the community dance. After Mom left the farm, Don quit his job there and aggressively pursued a relationship with her. I'm sure it was easy for Mom to enjoy his soft and tender charm. He expediently divorced his wife, leaving her and his four children to survive on welfare, and set out to become my proud new stepfather. I didn't mind too much. It kept Mom occupied and off my back, and it seemed to make her happy, so I encouraged the relationship.

Dad was soon intimately involved with a widow who had been a longtime friend of the family. Her name was Roma. She had a daughter and son-in-law, Beverly and Will, who lived with her and disapproved of the relationship. Beverly and Will made a lucrative and prestigious living at showing, selling, and breeding champion quarter horses. While Dad and Roma courted, Billy was taken under Will's wing who began to groom him as a winning contest rider. I was always excited to get to accompany them to a horse show and watch with enthusiasm while Billy dashed around barrels and darted in and out of a line of poles, trying to beat his competitors' time. All the while, Will began to make time with me!

Will was a handsome man, thirty-something and in an unhappy marriage. I was twelve. The sweet aroma of baled alfalfa, molasses-mixed oats, and sweat-drenched, leather saddles filled the air in his spacious, modern stable. There were several stalls lined on each side of the alleyway. Each one was home to a beautiful, noble stallion or a gentle mare. Quavering, high-pitched, horse-talk carried on day and night. Will and I began to meet in the tack room, as he cautiously negotiated an affair with me. I was more than happy to cooperate. The relationship enabled me to be near my brother and Dad, while enjoying special, yet malignant attention. Long horseback rides in the woods provided opportunity and privacy for a progressive sexual relationship. Will knew I was a virgin, and he seemed to relish the sport of slowly, yet strategically bringing me to succumb to his seduction. I was still afraid of intercourse, even though my revolting behavior had easily ascended me to third base and then had me trying to steal for home. Billy became suspicious of us and confronted me. I denied that anything was going on. I was worried that this could somehow destroy his opportunity for fulfillment, and he didn't deserve me ruining things for him. I began to look for a way out. Soon after, I misstated something that revealed to Beverly that things weren't quite as innocent as I had hoped they appeared. She cornered me, I lied, and I later broke it off with Will. Dad and Billy continued to travel to horse shows with Roma, Will, and Beverly every weekend and sometimes through the week. Being unable to accompany them, I lost contact with my brother and missed seeing him become a man.

Boys were pining for Cindy and me to show them attention. The slightest glance or mannerism that we might throw out unintentionally, or purposefully, would arouse them to a fiendish, hormonal reaction. Cindy was unofficially engaged to David Johnson, a guy who had already graduated from high school and was working out of town. Their roller coaster relationship left her insecure and tempted her to fall for cute guys with souped up, hot rod cars. Cindy, Tamera Gossett, and I began to run the streets like whores. Cindy played the ever-wise protector that kept the sex-crazed guys at arms' length. Tamera fell for any viper that hissed just right. And I? Well, let's see. I was pretty enough, malapert, and profoundly lost inside. I teased the boys but never allowed myself to go "too far." That seemed okay.

Mom was still trying to drag Cindy and me to church every Sunday. Most of her family faithfully attended meetings there, and they were a strong support for her. At the time, I found some of them to be self-righteous and verbally offensive. Mom had eight sisters, which amounted to a lot of cousins, all who appeared to enjoy a harmonious home life and couldn't possibly understand my plight. Brother Walter Duncan had retired, and a new preacher stood at the pulpit. He was eager to revamp and energize the church, which took money . . . our money . . . and he wanted it. But the biggest issue was the condition of my soul. Like sleepy eyes painfully squinting at dawn's first bright light, my black uncontrolled spirit cringed in the presence of the light and truth of Jesus. Discomfort during pointed sermons gave way to gnarling fury and led to horrendous arguments between Mom and me concerning my attendance with her in church. I usually won such encounters, and Mom tearfully left me in the snare.

*   *   *   *   *

The summer of '74 was tumultuous. I had twice attempted suicide and felt undone. Our landlord was threatening to kick us out of the trailer park because "we" were causing too much trouble. My friends and I congregated in front of my trailer, being loud late at night and drag racing up and down the street. The guys would rev their engines, while the girls playfully squealed and hollered at all the smoke and power under the hood. The police would often drive by and tell us to dissipate, but we would simply find a new place to gather. Sometimes the cops would escort us to our door, but that was equally unsuccessful in breaking up the ruckus.

Frank was a part of the gang, a 20-year-old kid who liked to hang out with us. I allowed him to get close to me, and I enjoyed having someone to talk to privately. It was another physical relationship that always stopped short of intercourse. Frank gave me a white fuzzy rabbit, and to my surprise, Mom allowed me to keep the rabbit and his cage inside. I named the rabbit Frankie, and he became a close friend as well.

A boy who lived in a house behind the trailer court was Billy Baker. I befriended him despite his painful handicap of stuttering and annoying childish antics. He was a gang member wanna-be who still rode his bicycle and cried when he got mad. Billy Baker didn't like me being alone with Frank, and he didn't like me brushing him off when he wanted the same attention all the other guys received. Billy Baker's criminal behavior began that summer, and I was the unknowing catalyst to his actions. He broke into our trailer and pointlessly ransacked it. He admitted to doing it, but Mom chose to take no legal actions. I patronized him, hoping it would be enough to get him to leave us alone. A few weeks later an arsonist sneaked into our "tin-can" home, which I depised, and set fire to everything we owned.

I was at Tamera's trailer when the fire engine came roaring up the street. I felt indifferent as we watched it turn the corner and head up the street toward my section of the trailer park. Then Tamera and I instinctively took off running after it. Far down the street, I saw orange flames dancing from the windows of my trailer, as if they wanted to be free but couldn't sever themselves from the base that provided sustenance. The landlord, a once strong man, was feverishly spraying water into the windows with his garden hose. His legs were spread far apart, the front leg bent forward . . . the back leg taut and providing the brace for a determined lunge of attack. The water hose was drooping heavily midair, as was necessary to stretch the needed distance. He relinquished his position when the fire engine pulled into place and firefighters began their own assault. Black, pungent smoke surged from every opening, even from between the riveted sheets of metal that encased the trailer. The windows took turns popping and exploding. Shattered glass resembled the spraying water as it sailed high into the air and far into the street and yards. People were gathered around, looking sorry. Mom was at my Aunt Kay's farm picking blackberries. I ran to call her. When she arrived, the fire trucks were still dousing our shell of a home, but the flames had long been extinguished.

We stayed with friends and family for several days. Mom was feebly clutching to stability. Getting her through the crisis was more important to all of us than the loss of our home and possessions. The day came when we needed to go back and inventory the damage.

The arsonist had started separate fires in two locations: on a living room stuffed chair and on Cindy's bed. The fire in the bedroom had self-extinguished. The only remaining evidence was a small four-inch burnt circle in the worn and faded bedspread that had once decorated my bedroom in our family home. All the fire damage was confined to the connected living room and kitchen. The drapes were gone, and the cheap wall paneling was either burned away or charred. The carpet had melted into tiny, black, hard balls. The kitchen cabinet doors were made of molded plastic with metal hinges and a handle in the center of each door. The intense heat had caused the cabinets to melt. They looked like crumpled paper mysteriously suspended from the ceiling and held in place by hinges that still functioned properly. Glassware and utensils were in tact, but the horrific smoke had spoiled all the food. Most photographs were melted and destroyed. Mom's clothes and mine were kept in the back bedroom and fortunately the closet door was closed, so we were able to wash out the choking odor of smoke from most of the clothing. The majority of Cindy's clothes however, were unsalvageable. We were amazed the television still worked though charred. Pathetically, we returned to our seared shelter to live. I think it was the very same night President Nixon resigned from office. Frankie the rabbit had miraculously survived the fire and was now quite satisfied . . . he was allowed free reign inside until we decided what to do next.

The FBI (or KBI) was called in to investigate the fire. They thought I was a troubled teenager (I was) and for some reason had set fire to my own home (I didn't). A series of interrogation meetings began. I found it amusing until I realized that most people, including my mother, shared the same opinion as the law enforcement officers. A date was set in mid-August for me to take a lie-detector test. Mom responsibly delivered me to the authorities who were waiting in the landlord's cool, comfortable, rental office. I remember the soothing feeling of being in an air-conditioned room, in contrast to our small, hot mobile home. Two, suited men exerted little effort in making me feel at ease. They proceeded to place me in a chair with wooden armrests. A Velcro-strapped gadget was placed around my waist and wrists. I was given something tubular to hold in each hand. It reminded me of the electric chair, and I made a mental note to not allow myself to end up there. Supple, black-coated wires attached all the devices to a machine that rested on the landlord's office desk. It was just like the movies . . . little, free-motioned, arms squiggled busily as they left a trail of inked peaks and hopefully the truth. I was asked to sit completely still and answer with only a "Yes" or "No." One of the men sat with a pen in his hand and made marks on the resulting printout as the other man asked me questions. As a test, they asked if my name was Connie Littleton . . . "yes."

"Do you live in Olive Hill, Kentucky?" . . .

"Yes."

"Have you ever smoked marijuana?" . . .

"No."

The man at the desk made a mark on the paper. They continued to drill me, asking silly questions between very serious questions. It wasn't a game. They were purposefully wearing me down and trying hard to prove I was guilty so they could pack up and go home.

"Did you set fire to your home?" . . .

"No."

". . . To your Mother's home?" . . .

"No."

". . . To your Father's home?" . . .

(Hey, I mused, they did their homework! After all, it was suppose to be Dad's home, not ours!) . . . "No."

"Do you know who did?" . . .

Cautiously I answered "no." It seemed I had exasperated them, and they decided to quit. With frustration and disappointment, they unhooked me from their toy. I hoped I was free, but they persisted with their digging. We spent a great deal of time discussing the results, and I was asked to elaborate on several points. I sorrowfully shared my view of Billy Baker, and my suspicion of his guilt in this crime. I was impressed with their rectangular, little black box. It accurately deciphered all my answers except one. The machine determined I lied about having smoked marijuana. Unfortunately that happened near the beginning of the session, so the detectives concluded

I was lying about other things as well. I never *had* smoked marijuana! I had been with friends when *they* were, but I didn't participate. Eventually, I was exonerated, and as far as I know, nothing else became of it.

Chapter Four

(The following chapter contains graphic content that may be inappropriate for some readers.)

I secretly hoped Mom and Dad would be able to mend their differences, but that became an increasingly ridiculous notion. Every time they got near each other, a fight would break out. Most of the time they limited the scene to red-faced screaming, but many times one or the other couldn't resist taking a swing, attempting to add the right punch to their point. Then they would become a tangled mess of fury, just like the snarling wild dogs that fought so fiercely outside our garage door only a few years before. We kids would stand by pleading, crying, or trying anything to break it up. I was beginning to see how cruel Dad could be, and I began defending Mom more readily. For her years of hard work on the farm, she received little or nothing by way of alimony. An occasional child support check would be handed over as though it were a great favor. Then to everyone's astonishment, Dad began construction on an elaborate new home he claimed to be for Roma.

Mom and Don quickly decided to marry and move to Mansfield, Ohio. I would attend my eighth grade year in a huge, inner-city school. They purchased a common, inexpensive, new, two-bedroom trailer house. Cindy had graduated from high school and decided to attend Kentucky Christian College in Grayson, Kentucky. Somewhere amidst all the commotion, she had managed to find Jesus. I sneered at her conversion but inwardly hoped for her success. I had watched Mom and Dad fight for years over the Bible and its real meanings. I had seen them sit with opened Bibles on their laps, yelling and pointing to the text. One night back in the house on the hill, I had watched Mom as she bolted from her seat and threw her Bible at Dad with vigorous aim. Thin pages fluttered in the air before it hit Dad's leg and slid to the floor and plopped upon the wall-to-wall carpeted floor of our then stylish quarters. I think that was a deciding moment for me. God was the topic of an argument, and I wanted nothing to do with Him.

I hated moving out-of-state and leaving Dad and Billy, but I hardly saw them anymore as it was. Of course, I dreaded leaving my friends, but Tamera and I had started shoplifting for kicks, and our beguiling delinquency was evolving into downright criminal actions. I knew I needed a fresh start, and I hoped this was it. Frank and I were still close, as our friendship had grown *completely* platonic. It helped when he found another misfit that more obligingly consummated his sex drive. I still had Frankie the rabbit, and he would accompany me to my new surroundings but would need to remain outside the new trailer.

Mom's wedding was to be held in my Aunt Joann's country home, and her husband, Uncle Harold, would officiate the ceremony with his hillbilly drawl and reassuring smile. I had forgotten the appointment and was snatched from Tamera's yard as we sped off to the event. I walked into a stuffy room lined with inconvenienced faces. There I stood realizing my clothing was grotesquely inappropriate. I had on a tight T-shirt and even tighter cutoff, blue jean shorts. My buttocks squeezed indecently from beneath the white ravels that fringed the French-cut garb. Aunt Kay grabbed me as she protested my attire and shoved me onto the couch. She quickly seized a pillow and placed it over my lap, in an effort to hide my shameful nakedness. The "I dos" were said, the bride was kissed, and we were out of there in less than an hour. Mom and Don dropped me off at Tamera's trailer where I rejoined the gang and carried on as if nothing had happened.

A few weeks later we were on our way to a new state of residence. I was extremely excited and determined to rediscover the "good girl" that I hoped was still inside. We moved just a few days before school began in Ohio. Mom had sewn a new outfit for me to wear the first day of school but hadn't found time to press the freshly stitched seams and hem. We arrived in Mansfield the night before school commenced and rented a cheap hotel room close to the rundown school I would soon be attending. The room was undecorated and had dirty, old-fashioned, checkerboard floor tile. A disagreeable odor hung heavily in the stagnant air.

Mom helped me lay out the raiment for my debut the following day. It was made of ribbed, double knit, green-and-white checked fabric and smelled new and pleasant . . . just the way I hoped to appear to the prospective friends I would face the approaching morning. Since an iron was not accessible, we decided to place the hem of the pants under some heavy objects, in hopes that it would be pressed flat by morning. I was surprised, but pleased at Mom's attention to detail *and me.* I hopped into bed with newfound expectancy.

The rented room was a suite of sorts. It had two beds with a flaking, stucco wall between them, connected by a large, open archway. It felt unnatural, perhaps even vulgar, to see Mom and her excited, new husband climb into the same bed. I stared sleeplessly at the lightbulb hanging alone from the smoke-stained ceiling. A few feet away, just out of sight, the newlyweds played and giggled between weakly attempted hushes. Mom's muffled moans under her husband's commanding grunts made me ill and breathless. My heart pounded with tormenting confusion.

The first day of my eighth grade school year was uneventful. I don't remember anything about it except how cutesy and hick I felt in the homemade outfit. Our trailer was parked in a fairly nice court with blacktop driveways and a Victorian streetlight on each lot. The electricity to our mobile home was turned on quickly, but the Gas Company moved more slowly at getting us connected. The cook stove and furnace were fueled by natural gas, which meant little or no cooked meals or heat. Mornings were starting to get chilly as Mom and Don continued to look for work, so far without success. They both remained in bed each morning as I readied myself for school.

One morning was unusually cold as I tried to wake myself and trudge to the small bathroom where an electric heater and a closed door would keep me warm. I placed a pastry on top of the heater to warm while I sponge bathed (no hot water) and dressed. Despite the crisp morning, I decided to wear a thin, white, tennis top and great-fitting jeans. I was starting to figure out the acceptable fashion at school, and I was sure this would be a hit. I ate my meager, still-cold breakfast and had plenty of remaining time before I needed to walk to the bus stop. I decided to crawl into bed beside Mom to relax and keep warm. Trying to be unobtrusive, I quietly curled up next to her over-weight, warm body. She never acknowledged my presence, and I was relieved I hadn't disturbed her rest. Don rolled over to face Mom and stretched out his left arm over her body as in an embrace. That landed his hand right on my breast! I froze, mortified as he began to fondle me. My mind whirled, "Dear, God! Does he know what he's doing!?! Maybe he thinks I'm Mom. What do I do now?" I realized he was being very meticulous at keeping still the defiling arm, as it was lying across Mom's chest, and he didn't want the motion to awaken her. I started to squirm away, but he clinched my closest breast as if telling me to be still. I fearfully rolled my head in his direction. Over my mother's sleeping body, I saw him, with the side of his face burrowed in his pillow, look at me with one open eye. He arched his eyebrow into a question as a languid grin barely hid his black, rotting teeth. His expression asked me if I liked it. I jumped out of bed and ran to catch the bus. I never wore that top again.

Don claimed he spent his days filling out job applications and following up at places of employment. Mom got a job that was quite a distance away, which meant she left early for work and returned home late. For my birthday, I received a clock radio with an alarm. We were extremely tight on money, so I appreciated Mom's sacrifice in order for me to have a nice gift. Each morning the radio would softly click on and broadcast the day's news and top hits while I got ready for school. Mom would already be gone and, hopefully, Don would stay in bed . . . but not always.

At the beginning of the abuse, Don was apologetic. I actually felt sorry for him and wanted to help him. In no way did I desire his sexual attention . . . that would have been easy enough to gain elsewhere . . . but I truly believed he just couldn't help himself. As bizarre and unbelievable as it may seem, I didn't know what was really happening. I can't explain it. I knew about sex, but what he was doing didn't seem to be that thing called "sex." The whole time I thought I was the one confused, and someday I would wake up and understand the whole scheme of things and realize this was normal and all 13–year-old girls were expected to allow their fathers to practice sex with them.

Don slept in a pair of thin, raggedy, insulated longjohns that were at least eight inches too short for his six-foot frame. Most mornings he would punctually join me in the kitchen while I attempted to make my usual toast and jelly for breakfast. He would follow me like a haunting shadow. If I turned to exit the room, he would step in front of me and try to talk to me in a cooing tone about him and his sexual needs and how important I was to him. He pretended to care deeply about each scrap of dialog I offered up as conversation. Although never actually having "intercourse" with me, this vile creature committed numerous other hideous and unthinkable acts of violation against me. I felt disgusted and filthy and was plagued by the constant memories of these sexual assaults. Only by the grace of God was I able to continue on with any kind of a normal life.

I didn't do well in school. Cheerleading tryouts were a joke. It was politically ordered, and I didn't meet the criteria. Right away a girl (now that's a loose term!) chose me as the recipient of her "wimp of the year award" and began stalking and harassing me. A lot of energy was exhausted on dodging her, until I finally grew tired of the chase and turned to face her. I tried to fight back, but I always got beat up and defamed. It's funny, but, in some twisted way, her attacks became entertainment. I think the game of threats and bruises distracted my thoughts from home. There were a few nice kids and a couple of teachers who befriended me that year in school, but for the most part, it was all a waste of time.

I got mononucleosis and missed three weeks of school, which limited any hope of making good grades. That was unimportant. What bothered me most was the doctor from whom I received treatment. You guessed it! I have a sore throat, and he tells me I need a breast and vaginal exam. There was no nurse in the room when I stripped down to nothing, unaware of his intentions. He examined me, more for his own well being than mine. It didn't hurt and it didn't matter. Nothing mattered. I felt like dirt and didn't desire to live. Surely I didn't even deserve to live . . .

Perhaps to patronize me, Don confided in me as though I were his best friend. He told me about the day at the egg factory when we had the dance and found the office destroyed. Evidently, Dad caught him and Mom having sex in the front office. Don relayed to Mom his confession to me, which prompted her to present me a quick, indignant denial. I silently abhorred her irrelevant and empty broadcast of innocence, as my respect for her was nearly nonexistent. I couldn't imagine how she didn't know what Don was doing, so therefore, in my child's mind, she must condone it.

I played detective and discovered that Don was lying to Mom about his short-lived employment. He told her he got laid-off, but in reality he had quit. Mom and I were fighting severely. She sometimes pulled my hair or beat me while slinging me across the room. I *never* hit her back. I tried to stay at a friend's house until she came in from work, in order to stay clear of Don. That got me in trouble, and I was called a whore for running the streets late. I then began taking the bus home after school, and if I saw that Don was inside when I arrived at the trailer, I pulled back the underpinning of the trailer and crawled underneath. That's where Frankie the rabbit lived, so he and I visited until Mom came home. Many times the snow was deeper than the bottom of the trailer, which was at least eighteen inches from the ground. It was a terribly bitter winter that year and there seemed to be no end in sight. One dreary evening I came home and found my rabbit had frozen to death.

I considered lying there beside him until the same thing happened to me. Instead I began to devise a plan.

Don must have sensed I was going to tell on him. I had come home from a friend's house after dark and figured I was in trouble. All the lights were out and Mom was sitting in her rocking chair in the living room, crying. Don was on the floor below her, kneeling in a humble, sympathetic fashion. He had told Mom that he had played with my breast *one* time, and he was sorry. He explained that he did it for my own good. He felt I was becoming too interested in boys, and he wanted to make sex look dirty in my mind. So he did this to show how ugly sex is and that I shouldn't have any part of it. Mom fell for it. She went into her bedroom (with him), and there they remained for days. She wouldn't talk to me other than scorning me. She later told me Don's behavior was my own fault, that I shouldn't have walked about the house without having on a housecoat.

Despite Mom's tearful objections, I moved out the end of that school year. Dad's new home was completed, and he and Billy were living there in great style. Dad slyly made sure he furnished a bedroom in my favorite colors and fashion . . . just in case I ever wanted to come live with him. So I did.

Chapter Five

Dad and Roma had broken up, and Dad found another lady from his church organization to marry him. I was in the wedding but never knew her beyond that day. She was married to Dad for a few months, just long enough to do some spiteful, mean things to Billy and steal some money. The last I heard of her she was in an asylum for the mentally insane. So Dad was a single man, pretending to be wealthy, feeling virile and alone. That meant he was gone from home nearly every night, either on a business or personal pursuit.

Billy was sixteen and already heavily involved in drugs and alcohol. I was glad to be back in Kentucky and in school with my brother and able to keep an eye on him. I was a freshman, talented cheerleader, popular, pretty, and well dressed. The star basketball player, Jeff Opner, and I were the hottest couple in school. Things were finally looking up!

When children are left unattended, they do stupid things. I was fourteen and thought I was in love. Jeff bought me an engagement ring, and we made plans for a fairytale wedding. One winter night, in front of his fireplace (with his parents in the next room!), I gave way to nature and lost my purity. It was nice. I deeply relished the *love* part. The relationship continued and grew for two years. He escorted me to ball games, cheerleading practice, medical appointments, and wherever I went, he usually took me. Jeff and I attended church together, and he taught me how to drive and cared for me when I was sick. We became soul mates as well as playmates.

Jeff and I had our own bedroom in the basement and spent many hours there alone. If Dad needed to interrupt us, he would always make sure he gave us time to be dressed or not caught in a shameful position. Once when he *did* catch us, he chuckled and said, "That's okay, I was young once too." Dad's attitude toward women is that they are for the male species to enjoy and to lessen his load in life (cook and clean). He seemed proud to provide the human rat race a beautiful specimen (me) for the plundering. I did indeed cook and clean for Dad and Billy. Regardless of my young age, I was the woman of the house. I cooked all the meals, washed dishes, did laundry, vacuumed, shopped for groceries . . . I did everything considered a woman's job. Many times on Saturday or after school, Dad would make me help in the egg factory or ask Jeff and I to make emergency egg deliveries. It seemed I could never do enough for Dad. I tried hard to please him, but he often yelled and scolded me for not keeping up with the house. It seemed as though Dad simply disliked me. Despite my heavy load of responsibilities at home, I maintained good grades in school and also practiced gymnastics and acrobatics several hours nearly every day.

Billy was partying his life away. Sometimes I would try to lecture him on the dangers of alcohol and drugs. Other times I would give him money to buy beer. His friends were in and out of the house a lot and often made fun of his little sister, but usually they tried to get me to go party with them. His closest buddies were Donny and Jamie. They lived within walking distance, and we had all been friends since an early age. I was starting to bore of my lifestyle and was getting antsy for something more exciting. Jeff graduated from high school before me, which left me feeling out of place. We grew distant from each other and eventually split up. It was painful for him, but I was glad to be moving on.

I had been a cheerleader for eight years and was tiring of my athletic friends. Patti was one of them. She and I were best friends during our junior and senior years in high school. Patti had a boyfriend who was quite older than her. He lived in an apartment in town where they often met. His best friend was one of my schoolteachers. Let's call him Teacher. I knew Teacher was interested in me. A girl has a way of knowing such things. He was also one of our coaches, which meant he was always around during the road trips and on the athletic bus. There were lots of opportunities to exchange glances and pass the hint that a fire was kindling. He was blonde, blue eyed, muscular . . . and married with small children. Patti arranged for him and me to get together at her friend's apartment. We met there several times, and social sex quickly sparked between us. A friend of his wife slashed my tires one night while we were together. She finally called the wife and told her how to catch us red-handed. When his wife knocked on the door and yelled his name, I ran and hid in the closet as he went to the door. A heartbreaking scene took place, but I wasn't discovered even though she walked into the room, turned on the light, and said, "I know she's in here." I think that in her heart she didn't want to find me or see me, because that would have made it too real to face. That was the end of our fling and a turning point in my behavior.

Dad's financial problems were getting more serious, and his accountant was around the office quite a bit. I suppose he found me irresistible, since he took a great chance in forcing himself on me just outside Dad's office. I pushed him away and learned a powerful lesson: the sting in the words, "I'll tell."

During school I had maintained a good GPA and kept up good attendance, but that changed during my senior year. I abruptly quit cheerleading (a shock and disappointment to practically everyone). I was tired of the grueling practices and long game nights. We were the only school in the state to have a boy cheerleader. I personally wasn't bothered by his homosexual lifestyle, but since we were close friends, it made the way for a lot of harassment I didn't want to deal with. The other girls on the squad, perhaps in response to my own vulgar reputation, started ignoring me or calling me names. Putting it all together, cheerleading lost its appeal. I struggled to pass required courses as my absences outweighed my attendance. Another teacher (married) was making advances toward me. . . . school was the last place I wanted to be.

Billy graduated the same year Jeff did and was hanging out with a *very* wild crowd. He had a conversion van with swivel chairs, small, round tables, and a tiny refrigerator. The outside was painted with an elaborate, detailed Indian on a horse with a setting sun and desert scene in the background. It was a party van and the coolest ride in town.

*   *   *   *   *

Dad married Wanda, his third wife, in June of 1978. She was a good woman and loved Dad with all her heart. I was glad to be relinquished of my duties in the house, but it caused me to feel unneeded. They were newlyweds and enjoyed their privacy, which meant I was encouraged to stay out of the house. Right away, they were expecting a baby.

Dad was still pastoring his church but having a lot of problems from the leaders. His denomination didn't believe in divorce except for reasons of adultery, and then one was not allowed to remarry. He convinced them Mom *was* adulterous, and a wicked harlot, therefore justifying their divorce. Now he had to figure a way to be allowed to marry Wanda and still keep his pastorate (it paid no salary, but was a serious ego booster for him). Somehow he pulled it off, but most of the congregation left the church. It didn't take long for Wanda's swollen belly to announce their accomplishment. Dad was nearly thirty years her senior, and the circumstances were scandalous. One Sunday afternoon, Wanda was crying and proceeded relaying to me the events that transpired that morning in church. Unbelievably, one of the leaders of the congregation started an argument during the sermon and pulled a knife on my father. Dad watched as the man eventually raged out of the building, but stopped suddenly next to Wanda's pew. "This is all your fault!" he spouted at Dad's young, naïve, hopeful, expectant wife. Some years later that man took his own life with a handgun.

Mom and Don moved around several times and went from job to job. She finally left him, but not until she had gruesome bruises inside and out. High on marijuana and speed, in the wee hours of the morning, I knocked on my mother's door, having decided to tell her everything her husband had done to me. It was a weary scene. I told the story I had rehearsed hundreds of times. She listened, offered no comfort, and dismissed me. I don't remember her hugging me or supporting me in any way, but then again, I *was* stoned. Perhaps I can't remember.

With Mom back in town, it meant she and Dad would butt heads more often. Billy and I tried to keep them apart, and usually it worked. Once Mom came to visit me at Dad's, so I quickly met her outside the door and stood there on the steps exchanging polite dialogue. An argument started over something (it didn't take much), and I was tiring of the scene. About that time, Wanda came to the door and said I was wanted on the phone. Mom thought Wanda told me to come inside in an attempt to rescue me from my screaming mother, so Mom lost it! She drew back her hand and started for Wanda. I had to physically hold her back from hitting a woman at fullterm pregnancy. I yelled, "What's wrong with you?" Mom was furious and spouted, "She's not telling you to come in! You're *my* daughter! I'll talk to you any way I want!" I got it cleared up without a catfight, but it was exhausting.

Billy and I shared the same "druggie" friends and went to wild parties together. The drug scene is a realm of false reality like no other. Many nights were spent standing in a stupor around a campfire, holding a beer, and passing joints. I "dropped" a lot of acid: mescaline, orange sunshine, Mr. Bill . . . it came in a lot of names. I snorted heroine, angel dust, speed, and cocaine. I spent nearly every night for a year passed out in somebody's van or on a stranger's floor. My favorite place was the woods. It was often far away from the law or homeowners. Perhaps twenty or more vehicles would pull up around a makeshift fire, somebody would turn up their stereo, and we would be set. The Rolling Stones, AC DC, Cheap Trick, Van Halen, Lynyrd Skynyrd, and my favorite, Bob Segar, rocked us into oblivion. Billy and I helped each other stay safe and alive. We were best friends. Even though it was a pointless, confusing era, it was a special time with my brother that I will cherish forever.

I decided one night to run away. I packed a bag and took off hitchhiking. I made it all the way to Nashville, Tennessee,

over six hundred miles. I can't tell you why I did it, just searching, I guess. I actually made some good acquaintances. One
guy was a social worker, he gave me money and tried to get me
to call home. Another guy was a trucker who gave me a ride
after I had no sleep for more than twenty-four hours. I was
nodding off but knew it was imperative to stay awake for safety's
sake. He told me to sleep, that he wouldn't hurt me. I did rest,
and not even a hint of advancement was made toward me.

In Dad's warped logic, he felt it allowable for Billy and I
to host parties in our house. He felt better knowing we were
there instead of on the roads. We had a large, open basement
with a pool table, dart board, fireplace, and restroom. All the
needed elements for a great party! Sometimes over a hundred,
stoned freaks would stagger into our house. Many times we
never even knew who they were. I had a lot of good friends that
loved me because I could party as late as they could, or because
I loved to laugh or listen to music and dance. Sex became less
of an issue, although plenty of it still took place. My closest
circle of friends and I had a kinship, like brothers and
sisters . . . hound-like sexual behavior would have ruined it.
Several of them were eventually killed in accidents or shot in
drunken brawls. I could tell you numerous stories of how close
I came to being one of them, dead and spending eternity in
Hell.

It wasn't unusual to be at somebody's house getting high
and have the police called by a neighbor to calm us down or
run us off. One of our least favorite state policemen was T.R.
Jade. He was a big man with a mean, authoritative voice and
stance. He particularly disliked me. One time, at a party he
tried to bust up, he attempted to arrest me for prostitution. He
said he saw me through the window with a nightgown on.
(Now I've never been in a whorehouse, but I don't think they
sit around in lingerie!) The entire time, I was sitting on the
arm of a chair beside some guy and was laughing and talking
like normal. There was no sex going on anywhere in the
house . . . that just wasn't our scene. We were a bunch of worn-
out hippies, too tired or stoned to even *think* about sex. T.R.
pressed his point until my friends decided they had heard

enough. I don't know if there was another cop in the cruiser, but T.R. was alone with us in the house and about to get roughed up if he didn't leave. It cost us a lot of hassle in the long run, but I was extremely grateful for my friends sticking up for me, keeping me out of jail, and making T.R Jade tuck his tail and scoot down the road.

*   *   *   *   *

It was a quiet, Sunday night when a stranger banged on our front door. Wanda was reclined on the couch, gently holding her pooching, fullterm belly as Dad and I both answered the door. The moment he pulled back the elaborate, brass knob on the solid wood, colonial entrance, we understood the urgency behind the pounding knock. The egg factory was located directly across the highway from our stately residence. Flames were roaring high into the air from the back loading dock. In one breath Dad ran out the door and pleaded, "Oh, my God."

It was a long night for the firefighters and us. Only the front office was spared from flames, but it took a lot of heroic and determined action. The firemen left at dawn, then Dad and I walked around the building to survey the remains. We had a new Monte Carlo and a costly, refrigerated delivery truck parked in the docks. They were completely burnt to black, smoking frames. Nearly everything was smoldering, either charred or in ashes. Dad walked to a tree and vomited, while I helplessly waited to walk with him back to the house.

Billy and several of our partying friends got a job in a soup factory in northern Ohio. He rented a large house out in the country with several other guys who had started a rock n' roll band. Nearly every night the band had jam sessions while the groupies hung around getting wasted. I traveled there several times with friends and partied with them. The band was booked to play in a popular bar, and a couple girlfriends of mine and I wanted to go. My car had a dead battery, and I tried fixing it but to no avail. Finally, we decided to take off hitchhiking. There we were, four girls, each with a bag on our shoulder, and our thumbs out. We had no trouble getting rides. Around 4:00 A.M. we were dropped off on the country road that would take

us to Billy's house. Incredibly, I noticed my pants were disintegrating practically before my eyes! When I had been working
on my battery earlier, I had leaned it against my lower abdomen to carry. The battery acid took a while, but it sure did
destroy those jeans. Along the side of the road, I pulled another
pair of jeans from my bag and changed clothes. We walked up
to the house an hour later and found people crashed out all
over the yard and house. Billy was blitzed, but coherent enough
to scold us for being such "wild and crazy fools!"

In February, Wanda gave birth to an adorable baby girl
they named Anna Marie. Dad was proud, but I think he was
hoping for a boy. Spring was nearing, along with my high
school graduation. Dad bought me a new Firebird for my graduation present. It was beautiful and boosted my low self-esteem
and confidence. It made me feel equally attractive, rather high-
classed, not stuck-up, just above my unwholesome behavior. I
didn't allow drinking or smoking inside its velour capsule and
made sure its metallic, gold paint remained waxed and shiny.
Four days prior to the commencement ceremony, I was caught
in a torrential downpour. Though driving slowly, my tires hy-
droplaned and caused me to veer off the road and crash into a
concrete post. It was a simple, slow motion accident, but it
caused irreparable damage to my beautiful car. I crawled from
the wreckage and sprawled out on the ground like the crumpled
eagle on the hood of my once-gorgeous Firebird. The pelting
rain heckled my hopeless, crying heart, as I lay destitute in my
blood upon the ground. I refused to go to the hospital, as
traffic slowed to checkout the scene. I felt like a clown in a
Halloween horror flick . . . the villainess that deserved her ensuing, slow, torturous destruction. "Oh, well," I tried to convince myself, "It's just a car and more scars."

I had a lot of dreamy ideas for a career after high school,
but none seemed realistic. I was voted as "Most Beautiful" in
my class, but I never really thought I was all that pretty. I
enjoyed sewing and designing my own clothes, at least until I
got involved with drugs. I was thinking about trying to go to a
fashion college in Atlanta, Georgia, but I knew both Mom and
Dad were financially strapped, and there wasn't a likely chance

of that happening. On a whim, I requested information from Bauder Fashion College, specifically for Fashion Design and Modeling. It was one of those things a silly girl does while dreaming of a different life. It turned out that Dad and Wanda were at their wits end with me and would have done anything to get me out of their hair (at least that's how I felt). Wanda took care of getting financial aid for me through the school, and plans were quickly made for me to leave the end of the summer to attend one of the most reputable fashion colleges in the world.

My plans were big news at graduation. My red-neck class-mates were happy for me and hoped I would be able to settle down. Most of them weren't the partying type. I had rented a small trailer with a hard-core, partying friend, Janie Duncan, and we arranged to have the graduation party at our place. An hour before I walked across the stage to receive my diploma, I took a hit of acid. I was stepping high, smiling big, and on a "trip" when the caps and tassels were tossed into the air.

Janie and I didn't stay in that trailer for long. She loved to drink Wild Turkey whiskey, so one day we headed to the bootlegger and purchased a "fifth" of the vile poison. We went back to the trailer and spent the day drinking the entire bottle by ourselves. By evening some friends rolled in with another "fifth" of liquor, and we helped down it as well. Later more friends stopped by with a keg of beer in the back of their jeep and were heading to the lake, and we were invited to go along. Of course, we climbed in and took off. We were almost at the lake when Janie started feeling sick and needed to get out. I helped her get to the side of the road to lie down. The driver of the jeep had pulled off at the first available spot, which was on the left side of the road and made the mistake of keeping on his headlights. I flopped down on the ground beside Janie and stretched out while she was sitting up and losing her stomach. I heard something that made me glance toward the jeep. I caught the eye of one of my friends just as he was slowly closing his eyes and turning his head away from my direction. I knew that whatever was about to happen . . . he didn't want to see! I then looked directly past Janie to see a van coming right at us! Janie was hit first. Her sitting position entangled her under the vehicle with horrible crunching, mangling sounds. My face hit the bumper, and my body rolled over on its side. The van continued to roll over the hill until it crashed. Our friends ran to us right away, as one sped off to get help. The tire tracks from the van were inches from my feet and head. Miraculously, I was positioned perfectly between the wheels as the vehicle drove over us. I couldn't feel my legs, and my face was covered with blood. I repeated several times with gargling cries, as blood poured into my mouth and choked me, "I can't feel my legs, I can't feel my legs . . ." Fearfully, testing for sensitivity, one of my friends slowly grasped my calf and squeezed. He was more scared than I was, yet we were greatly relieved when I could easily feel his touch. I kept asking about Janie, and I could tell they weren't revealing to me the intensity of her condition and the situation. An ambulance finally arrived and took me to the hospital, and a helicopter came for Janie. I was released that night with a bandaged, swollen, and bruised face. Dad showed up to get me. He exhibited more anger than fear or relief. I had several stitches between my eyes but suffered no other consequences, except for the tiny, V-shaped scar, which dimmed my fantasies of a modeling career. Janie spent nearly a month in the hospital. Her condition was critical, as her spleen had ruptured and was removed. But she recovered, and for many years she continued to smoke dope and drink alcohol, a dirty trick to play on a body with no spleen.

Billy was increasingly worried for me. I suppose he knew he contributed to my habits and perhaps felt somewhat responsible. He gave me a silver necklace with a dove on it. On the back were inscribed the words, "Oh Holy Spirit Enlighten Me." It was completely out of character for him, and it significantly affected my opinion of him and life itself.

By August of 1979 I was transported to Atlanta, Georgia, by Dad and Wanda and bid good riddance.

Chapter Six

Bauder Fashion College, when I attended, had a dress code that supposedly instilled professionalism. Two-inch heels and dress clothes only . . . a major change in pace for me! I had several suitable pairs of shoes, and I was going to use my sewing machine to make some fashionable clothing. All my belongings were packed in Dad's van as we made a stop at the mall to pick up some things I would need for my newly acquired, suburban apartment. When we returned to the van, unbelievably, someone had stolen my sewing machine and boxes of shoes! Dad couldn't afford to replace them, so I was left with one pair of heels and a limited wardrobe to wear to a school full of snobbish, uppity, high-class students.

Living in my own apartment instead of a dormitory close to campus was a mistake. My commute required two transfers on the city bus and an hour's wait between stops—often in the rain or snow. I was sunk from the beginning. I had to get a job right away, so I got hired at a fast-food restaurant close to my apartment, but too far away to walk. Grants and loans provided school tuition, and occasionally Dad would send money for food or rent, but most of it was my responsibility. I could eat at work for half price, but even then I could rarely afford meals. Every ten minutes or so, the food is thrown away at most fast-food restaurants. My manager knew I was hungry, so she secretly allowed me to snatch food from the garbage containers and hide it in my bag to carry home for later. I had stale burgers and water for breakfast, lunch, and dinner.

I was way out of my element at school. I enjoyed the classes and modeling activities but never made a single friend in the eight months I was there. I had to work a lot of hours to fulfill my part of the financial demands, which forced me to skip classes. I met a girl at work who needed a place to live, so she moved in with me on the pretense of splitting the bills. Instead, she disappeared with my television and a few other valuables and left me owing more than my share.

I volunteered to help backstage with a fashion show at the school. I didn't enjoy being in front of the camera or on the runway, but I *did* thrive in the bustling, behind-the-scene aspect of such productions. I think it was at one of those shows where I met Byron. He was another cocky, handsome dude that made one believe he had something she needed. We dated a while and got fairly close, until he took me to his house one night for a party. There were lots of people in every room doing a lot of drinking . . . just another typical party scene. It was getting late and people were starting to dissipate. Byron asked me to come to the back room; he wanted to show me something. He opened the door to one of the bedrooms, disclosing naked, pulsating bodies tangled up in boorish acts I need not describe. I had heard of orgies but had never seen one. It was disgusting, and I was revolted at his invitation to join them. It took a while to get out of the house, but I did manage to stay clear of the gangbang.

I made a few good friends at the bus stops. Ben H. was some kind of an executive with a wife and four children. I guess he was a strange man, but he liked me and seemed okay to hang out with. He came to my apartment to visit, and many times he gave me a ride to school or work. (When it rained he drove, instead of riding the bus.) Once I got extremely sick and had no money or insurance for visiting a doctor. I kept an infection for months before he realized what was going on. He swept me off to the doctor's office, paid the bill, bought my medication, and continued to check on me until I was well. And this is the shocker . . . not once did he ever try or ask to kiss or touch me whatsoever. He was an honorable man with some personal problems, but inappropriate sensuality was not one of them.

Crystal was a pretty, black girl that rode the same bus I did every morning. She was younger than I was (I was eighteen) and made me laugh. We made plans to go visit The Underground Atlanta together. "The Underground" was built for protection during the Civil War and is now located in the downtown area. It's mainly a tourist attraction during daylight hours, but a few, mostly jazz bars, still operate there; and at that time, they attracted an undesirable, evening crowd. Of course, we had to take the bus, and we weren't sure where we were going. We got off at the wrong stop, walked around the corner, and found ourselves on a street lined with hundreds of black people. They were sitting and standing in hordes, swarming in and out of rundown, windowless buildings, and lined up along a concrete wall by which we needed to walk. I wondered if Crystal felt any alarm. I followed her through the crowd like a scolded pup. We were halfway there when a girl, large and ominous, stepped in front of me and stopped me. I looked up . . . she looked down. "Chalk don't walk this block," she snarled. "I'm sorry," I whispered. Crystal turned toward me and quickly said, "Keep walking." We made it to the Underground, and I still have the souvenir I purchased. Crystal and I have lost touch. Now, I can't remember her last name. I hadn't been around many black people until I went to Atlanta, so I feel fortunate to have spent time with her and to have learned more of the hardships that many blacks experience. The girl on the street that day is part of the racial problem, and Crystal is part of the solution.

The school's absentee policy required a one-letter grade drop with each four absences. I was quickly flunking out of school. I had changed my major to Fashion Merchandising, a two-year degree, instead of the four-year Fashion Design program for which I enrolled. However I remained a double major with Modeling as my second component. I was informed I had the percentage grade to pass but would not do so due to my excessive absences. Most of my modeling classes met later in the day, which allowed more time to prepare and arrive on time. Thus, my modeling grade stood sufficient for certification. I was terribly disappointed. I sincerely tried my best, but

I *had* to work, and that left little time for school. I skipped graduation, because I was afraid of embarrassment. They mailed me my Modeling certificate.

My failure there was the result of two problems: living too far away from the school (my poor judgement) and no money. Perhaps my parents did all they could. Mom took me shopping before I left for college and sent a mere twenty dollars during the entire year. I had saved some old and odd coins, which I took to the bank to deposit for the rent payment. The teller hardly knew what to do with the outdated pieces of metal, but we managed to come to an agreeable amount. I managed to keep myself in a shelter until Dad arrived with his van to load me up and take his disappointing daughter home . . . again.

I tried my hand at modeling for a career, but I wasn't a "natural," and I honestly didn't enjoy it.

Chapter Seven

I moved back home with Dad and Wanda for a short while. Anna needed to be moved out of the crib next to Dad and Wanda's bed and into her own room. Both Billy's and my room were vacant, and his was closer to the master bedroom as well as to a bathroom. They put Anna in my room, perhaps because she liked my purple carpet better than Billy's blue, and I slept in Billy's room. I felt very unwelcome and decided to move to Lexington, about eighty miles away. I still didn't have a vehicle, so Dad was gracious enough to help me. I found a duplex on a nice, shaded street in a decent part of town. My neighbors were a young couple with a little girl. My landlord was a smelly, old man who owned several properties in town. He helped me get a desk job down the street at a lumber company. He offered to hire me to dance in one of his bars as a stripper, but I declined. When I got close to being late on my rent payment, he suggested I have sex with him in exchange for the money due. I would have slept in a drainage pipe before I would have had sex with that nasty, old pervert!

I kept my job, despite the sexual advances from one of my co-workers, and kept up with my payments. There was a public pool and a nice city park a few blocks from my house. One lazy Saturday afternoon, I decided to go there to lie out in the sun. I had my spot established, was rubbed down with tanning lotion, and ready to kick back and relax. I happened to look over at one of the park benches, and a couple of young, good-looking guys dressed in suits were checking me out. I didn't mind; it struck me as the way courtship *should* be. A little later, two scummy hoodlums walked over to me and started a conversation. I should have bluntly sent them away, but that was a skill I hadn't yet developed. It was a mistake I would later regret. We visited a while, and in an effort to get rid of them, I made a monstrously, huge mistake. I told them where I lived! I looked over toward the cute guys . . . they were gone.

Much to my dismay, the "hoodlums" kept unexpectedly showing up. All that I knew about them were their names, Randall Curt and Randall Millner. How odd. I never knew where they lived. I suspected they sponged off whomever they could. For a while I was polite to them, unaware of how dangerous they were. They convinced me to go ride around with them in their beat-up, old, blue car. They bought some beer, and we drove to a lake outside of town. When I realized things were getting out of control, I got scared and asked them to take me home. They refused and started to get rough and loud. I decided it best to play along until I could get to safer territory, or maybe come up with a plan to escape. It was extremely hot, which I'm sure added to their restless, agitation. They shoved me back into their "heap" and set off cruising back toward a part of town where I would have never dared to go. It soon dawned on me that this was their home turf. It seemed normal in some ways. People were sitting on their porches, swatting flies, and watching their diapered, otherwise naked, children play near the street. Yet, an unexplainable fear gripped the pit of my stomach.

As I sat in the middle of my two adversaries, I began to pray that I would get out of there alive. They had already slapped me several times, pulled my hair, and bruised my arms from dragging me around and shoving me in and out of the car. It was all unnecessary because I was cooperating fully. It was like they were hyping themselves up for something. Something that I feared would undoubtedly involve me. A truck appeared in front of us loaded down with more scoundrels. As they drove by a house where lots of people were congregated, they started screaming obscenities and revving their engine. Just then, the light in front of us turned red. We stopped, and the truck in front of us sped off. A dark-complexioned man with unruly, black hair bolted up to our car. The window was down, and before we knew what was going on, he had a gun pointed directly at us. He was gripping it as tightly as fear was gripping my heart. The man was sweating profusely and had repulsive, evil eyes. Randall C., then the passenger, threw up his hands as if to say, "Don't shoot" and started talking fast. "It wasn't us, man! It was those idiots in front of us." I was surprised to hear him pleading. I nodded my head in agreement and tried to stay calm. He let us go and told us to stay out of his neighborhood. Both Randalls said they would. I think it must have shaken them up quite a bit because they took me home immediately after that. My prayer had been answered, but unfortunately, that was only the beginning of their terrorism.

Randall C. seemed to be the head of his gang. He brought his friends to my house and told them to stay there and make sure I didn't go anywhere. It was a stupid game but one they took very seriously. One time he posted a redheaded guy at my door, while he barged in and ruthlessly began destroying my few belongings. Randall M. and the redhead called him off. He was just about to kick the front of my television when Randall M. reminded him they could sell it, and he should leave it alone. I thought the tide may be turning in my favor, but the episode defied Randall C.'s authority and made him angry. They all left, without my television, and late that night Randall C. returned alone.

Randall C. was much stronger than I was, and I had no weapons with which to protect myself. He had been drinking but wasn't drunk. I tried to lock him out, but he broke the glass in the door, reached through the jagged hole and simply unlocked the knob. There was no use fighting. He held all my hair in one hand and dragged me to the bed. He commanded me to take off my clothes. Every time I hesitated or cried too loudly, he hit me with his other hand. He had my long, thick hair wrapped to my scalp, tightly around his fist. He struggled to undo his pants, while jerking my head and bending my neck backward with every move. My arms flailed wildly, and my back was steeply arched and in pain. I don't remember removing my clothes. I just remember him stretched out on top of

me, and how hard he tried to achieve satisfaction. He was very
fat and unable to accomplish his desired deed. He rammed his
huge body against anything obstinate until he was finally finished or simply gave up.

Strange how the mind works. Some things I remember
clearly about that terrible night, and other things I simply can't
recall. Perhaps I was knocked unconscious, I'm not sure, but
the only other thing I recollect was waking a few hours later,
right at dawn. The birds were singing to announce a misty
morning. As sweet as the music was which they sang, it was
not enough to erase the treacherous scene which consumed me
with a deep and wretched agony. It was an unusually chilly
morning, considering the hot summer we were having. My
neck and back ached as I struggled to alertness. My mind was
as foggy as the morning air outside my bedroom window. I was
numb and stone-faced as Randall C. limped his way out the
door, complaining as though each step caused him pain. I took
a hot bath and punctually arrived at work without mentioning
to anyone my previous night's horror.

I called the phone company and requested phone service.
I purchased the telephone but had to wait a few days before the
service would actually be connected. I hesitantly asked my neighbor to take me to the courthouse to file charges against Randall.
The law was of little help. They offered to issue a restraining
order against him, but that seemed futile. I borrowed a can of
mace from a friend and hid it under my pillow. I put a butcher
knife in my top dresser drawer. My landlord was angry that the
window was broken out and refused to fix it or install extra
locks as I had requested. He told me I would have to replace
the window myself, something I couldn't readily afford.

Temperatures exceeded one hundred degrees as I walked
home from my job at the lumber company. It had been a while
since I had seen any of Randall's gang, and I started to let
down my guard. I enjoyed a quiet night at home, watched a
late night TV show, and decided to go to bed. I had called the
phone company that day from work, checking on the progress
of my phone service. They said it would be the next day before
it would be working. Sometime that evening I was curious and

picked up the receiver. I was thrilled to hear a dial tone! There was a window at the head of my bed, so I placed a fan against the screen and pointed it toward my head. I hoped it would help me get some sleep. The trauma of being raped and the excruciating heat was wearing me out. I needed to rest so I wouldn't jeopardize my job.

The fan deafened my ears as it blew cool, night air over my restless body. I rolled over and for some reason opened my eyes. There at the foot of my bed stood Randall C.! He was swaying and reeking of liquor. I screamed and tried to jump out of bed. The knife in the drawer was my first thought, although I wondered if I would have the nerve to actually use it. It didn't matter; he was on top of me in an instant. He clasped one hand over my mouth, the other hand grasped around the back of my head. It felt as though he might break my skull. He said over and over, "I'm going to kill you b——. I'm going to f—— kill you right here." I was sure he would. He cursed me for a while and twisted me around in the bed like he was trying to get the feel of how to do it. By God's mercy, Randall decided to prolong his attempts and smoke a cigarette. With one hand, he reached into his shirt pocket and retrieved a cigarette and lighter. His other hand maintained a choking grip around the front of my throat. He placed the cigarette in his mouth, and out of habit, he released his hand from my neck to use it as a windshield around his mouth while he lit the cigarette. That was my moment. Freed from his grip, I thrust my hand under the pillow and easily retrieved the mace. Without hesitation, I pointed it just inches from his face and held down the sprayer. My determined expression and wimpy defense struck his distorted mind as comical. He laughed out loud like he appreciated the good joke. I continued to hold down the nozzle, keeping it pointed steadily toward his ugly, laughing face, emptying most of the container in a few seconds. It wasn't working. Horrified, I distinctly remember thinking . . . "Oh, God, I'm dead."

He knocked the mace out of my hand and started choking me. The joke was over, and he was angrily ready to carry out his plan. I struggled the best I could, frantically pulling at his huge arms and gasping for particles of air. Unexpectedly, *he* screamed and began digging on his own face! The mace had taken effect and was stinging his eyes and skin. I jumped out of bed and ran to the phone. I dialed 911 or the operator (I can't remember). He was bungling toward me, yelling and reaching to find me. A voice on the other end of the line acknowledged me. I fought panic as I quickly stated my address with a quivering, but determined-to-live voice. I spoke with distinct enunciation so as to be understood. I knew I had only a few seconds and wouldn't likely have the opportunity to repeat my location. She said something like, "What do you need?" I repeated my address and yelled, "Send the police!" just as Randall found the phone cord in the wall and jerked it loose from its connection. I prayed desperately that it would be enough to get help. Randall seized me again, and I started kicking, screaming, clawing, and swinging wildly . . . but with all my strength and careful aim. I was not going down without a fight. He realized he couldn't defend himself; the burning mace seemed to be intensifying rapidly. He gave up and started toward the door.

Outside he fumbled around as he found his car. Somehow he got the door open and perhaps from memory, backed out of the driveway and slowly made his way down the street. Just as he turned the corner, the police arrived. I tried to tell them the intruder had just left, and they could catch him if they hurried. The officer called on his radio and requested assistance, but he stayed there with me. I was annoyed and mentally scoffed his intelligence or allegiance to protecting society. Now looking back, I'm grateful he stayed with me and am sure it was the wisest move. I had sprayed so much mace that it got on my hands as well. I was sobbing and holding my face, which got the mace in *my* eyes. I can now wholeheartedly endorse its effectiveness . . . it *does* hurt!

I pressed charges and pushed the legal system to action. Randall was apprehended and spent a few days in jail. Then I got a letter requesting I come to a meeting with Randall and a mediator. It was some kind of conflict resolution program. I didn't go. Instead I moved back home to Dad's. For years, I never told anyone of the rape and assaults. Somehow I was *sure* I had asked for it. It would take nearly twenty years before the terror would leave me. I became a light sleeper and certainly could not sleep with a fan running. Hundreds of times I have startled from slumber when, in my mind, a nightmarish picture formed and froze in the darkness of night. There, at the foot of my bed, always to the right of center, a silhouette, looming wide with wiry hair and a bushy beard. It casts an odoriferous, gagging stench, wearing dirty jeans and a black t-shirt that exposes tattooed arms, and a sagging stomach. A man . . . a monster without a face . . . standing . . . looming . . . lurking at the foot of my bed while a roaring fan numbs my head.

I was convinced God was a part of getting my phone turned on a day early, just as I was sure he made Randall crave a cigarette in the middle of an intended murder. It started to spark a little hope in my spirit . . . that maybe there *was* some *good* reason for my existence. But, I wasn't ready to jump off the deep end and "accept Jesus," that was nonsense. But maybe . . . well . . . no . . . Jesus wasn't for me, I was too stained for that goody-goody religious crap. Like a director under pressure, storming aimlessly among to and fro actors, I declared, "On with the show!" Jesus slumped with a broken heart and let me have my way.

A few weeks later I heard on the news that two girls were found dead at one of the locations where the two Randalls had taken me. The scenario and evidence sounded familiar. I considered calling the authorities, but I was afraid Randall C. would find me and not only hurt me but little Anna and my family as well. I decided to keep quiet, a decision I have questioned time and time again.

Chapter Eight

It was nice to be back in a quiet, rural community, in a nice home with food on the table. Anna was growing into a cute, innocent little kid, and I enjoyed watching her. She was pure and kind. She didn't understand hate or lies. I spent hours staring into her clean, sweet eyes and wishing I could be there. I got a job at a department store and was quickly promoted to a managerial position and able to buy a car. Billy was attending college at a nearby state university and living in the dorms. Cindy had married and divorced once and was now dating a handsome man that appeared to be a good choice. On the whole, our family was settling down some, but the storm wasn't over yet.

Billy and I started partying together again. One night he got arrested for DUI and was put in jail, but they released him on his own recognizance, and he called me to pick him up. Several of his wild buddies were in the same cell and were released with him, so I agreed to take them all home. That was the first time I met my future husband, Harvey Kissick.

Harvey was the wildest of the wild. He rode a chopped out, 1956 Tiger Triumph, a collector's item. It had spoke wheels, chrome this and that, king and queen seats, sissy bar . . . all the bits and pieces needed to make it the envy of any hard-core biker. He was a machinist by day, drug dealer by night. I bought leather pants and a vest to wear on the bike with Harvey and obtained my own motorcycle license, though I rarely had the handlebars in my own hands.

I was now the cool chick that all the pimply-faced, dope-smoking high schoolers admired. They irritated me with their

childish beer parties and stupid grins. Using the needle was the
next and (Praise God!) last step I would take before waking up.

Running up, shooting up, mainlining . . . hooks the
body . . . and brings it down *fast*! I watched as my friends prepared the run, while another had his fingers gripped around my
biceps cutting off blood flow and trying to make my veins rise.
I kept my arm down and snapped my wrist several times, sometimes lightly smacking the inside of my elbow joint, preparing
a vein to rise up and take in the poison that would send me
away, perhaps for hours or days. Somebody else held a spoon
with water and the drugs mixed together (heroin, cocaine, speed,
etc.). They lit a cigarette lighter and held its flame under the
spoon until its consistency pleased them. Then using the sy-
ringe, they drew the potion out of the spoon and into the clear
tube and then slowly, so as to avoid a horrible rush, injected it
into my vein. We took turns: same needle; same kind of lost
fools!

The cops had been on our trail for quite a while. They
knew our vehicles and where we hung out. Several busts occurred, but they always came up dry. I remember one incident
when Billy literally carried me while running to get out before
we got arrested.

Billy, Harvey, and I had been to a concert when we drove
through town way after midnight. That was a mistake. In that
area nobody was on the streets late at night unless they were up
to no good. The cops briskly pulled us over, made us walk the
line, touch our noses, all that stuff, and then searched my car.
In the glove compartment was a full, forty-ounce bag of marijuana. One of the officers opened the bag of marijuana, looked
in, closed it, and returned it to the compartment . . . nothing
said. I hoped I got away with it (it *was* in *my* car and I would
be ultimately responsible), yet we were all carted off to jail. I
began imagining how the next few hours would play out . . . the
officer who stashed away the drugs would get me alone and
offer a hush trade in exchange for a sexual favor. I was already
trying to decide what I would do. But the arresting officer
disappeared. I think he was dispatched to another incident. I
was delivered to the jailer and after breathing into a Breathalyzer,

I was told to empty my purse. To my astonishment, a roach (that's slang for the butt of a marijuana cigarette) tumbled onto the table from the bottom of my bag! I was arrested for possession of marijuana and for public drinking. Billy and Harvey were arrested for public drinking, and Harvey was also arrested, for DUI. We were put in separate cells opposite each other. Somehow one of them got through with a joint in their pocket and a lighter. There was a broom next to their cell door, so Harvey lit the joint, passed it between Billy and him a few times, then slipped it into the end of the broom straw. Squeezing his arms through the small, food tray access hole, he precariously stretched the broom across the hall and held it there while I reached out and snatched the joint from within the bristles.

That night in jail I was having my menstrual cycle and had no hygiene products with me. There was a bunk with no sheets or pillow, just an army-type blanket folded at the foot of the bed. The toilet was a simple porcelain bowl with no lid, kind of like an outhouse. It was next to the door and in line of sight with the other cells' food tray opening. It was at times like these that my life seemed to be at the lowest possible point. Miraculously, the next morning they let us out and turned us loose, instructing us to walk back to where we were picked up. Though they could have impounded the car, it remained parked where we had been pulled over. Ironically, it was April Fool's Day.

Harvey and I ran up some cocaine and sat back to sweat out the rush before the high came, but the high never came. I started to crash, as we called it. That's a good name for it, because everything in me crashed at terrific speed into an unforgiving, invisible fortress. Everybody in the room was in a stupor. I looked at Harvey and quietly announced, "I'm dying." It wasn't nearly as dramatic to him as I was feeling inside, but he didn't laugh. I was sure I was finally dying and just wanted to let everybody know . . . maybe it would be something cool to watch . . . but it was okay with me to die alone, and especially okay to be dying. It was about time.

Morning light seemed deliberate in its unhurried arrival, but it did gradually break into the heaviness of that black night. That was the last time I shot up drugs. I drove home, packed my car with a few belongings, and headed out of town—just anywhere to get away from the crowd of people I called friends.

Harvey caught up with me and pleaded with me not to leave. He said he was tired of partying too and wanted to settle down. For hours he begged me to marry him and get a place to live, and together we would quit drinking and doing drugs. I wasn't really convinced it would work, but I figured I had nothing to lose. I was wrong . . . there was a *lot* more to lose.

We set the date for 2 May 1981. Our wedding "colors" were Harley Davidson emblems on black T-shirts and blue jeans. I wore a white blouse trimmed in black. The night before the wedding, Harvey's friends had a bachelor's party for him. It got out of hand, and several people ended up in the hospital, including our Best Man and Maid of Honor. We went ahead with the disgraceful ceremony. My brother and another friend stood up with us and signed the marriage certificate as witnesses. Harvey and I stood in front of the fireplace in Dad's formal living room with Dad positioned in front of us. His pastor's wedding book, the same one I've seen him use numerous times, was in hand. Several of our family members forced themselves to attend, and a few even brought gifts. Dad read us the wedding vows. We repeated them with clasped, nervous hands. Dad said, "You may now kiss the bride." Then he hung his head and walked away.

Wringing my hands, Harvey and I discuss
the wedding license with my father.

The bride had long lost her blush!

Chapter Nine

For a wedding present, Dad gave Harvey and me an acre of land. We borrowed a tent and lived there for at least a month. It was time to set tobacco, and Harvey was drafted to help. I got out of it for the time being to go to the doctor. My period was late, but that wasn't unusual. I was rarely regular, and a doctor had told me several years past that I wouldn't be able to bear children, something about an inverted uterus. I was ecstatic when the nurse told me I was at least four-to-six weeks pregnant! Harvey and I had been married less than a month; so I suppose I must have been pregnant before we married, although I had no clue of it, and it certainly wasn't *why* I married him. He took the news without much emotion, but we decided we needed to find a better shelter.

Dad still owned the house on the hill where I was raised as a small child, and it was vacant. It had been rented and was vandalized pretty badly. The previous renters also left a five hundred dollar electric bill unpaid, which meant the electric company wouldn't restore service until the bill was settled. Dad rented Harvey and me the house for a small amount, without electricity. That meant no cook stove or oven, no refrigerator, no lights, and no heat. I hesitantly moved in.

My pregnancy was coming along nicely, and I was starting to show. I quit drinking and doing drugs as soon as I found out I was pregnant, but I was concerned about the drugs I did before I knew of the pregnancy. I was sure I had done acid at least twice while pregnant, as well as a lot of drinking and smoking pot. I prayed my baby would be born normal and healthy.

There are few things I have sincerely claimed to hate. That house on the hill is one of them. As small children we heard strange noises there, like a wild animal or a woman screaming, and it was worse as a young adult! I'd see strange lights outside or hear scratching sounds. Worst of all, since the time I was ripped from there until many years later, I had nightmares that always took place in or around that house. Harvey continued to party with his friends while I stayed in the house alone in the dark. I kept a candle lit as much as possible, but gyrating shadows seemed to laugh at my fear. Evil lurked all around me, and I felt it. It started turning cold at night, and I convinced Harvey we had to make a change.

We rented a tiny trailer "by the week." Harvey had a good job, but we lived from paycheck-to-paycheck, so the arrangement was the best we could afford. Harvey was incarcerated for stealing and pawning a wedding ring from the bathroom of his workplace and then fired from his job. I was able to stay in the trailer while he was in jail, but we both knew it was time to get serious about our marriage and the baby, or both could be lost.

Harvey was a veteran from the Vietnam era. He never fought but served soon after the war ended. That earned him educational privileges under the GI Bill. It provided tuition and books and housing, as well as a monthly monetary supplement. He enrolled in college that fall, and we moved into the university's married housing. He did a fairly good job keeping up with the responsibilities at first. He made some friends in class that liked to party just as he did, so that kept him interested enough to keep up his attendance. In the meantime, I was excited to have a secure home for our baby that was coming soon, ready or not!

The baby didn't move a lot in my womb, but I wasn't sure how it was suppose to feel, so I tried to not worry. Of course when she *did* wiggle, it was very exciting for me. One time I grabbed Harvey's hand and placed it on my belly so he could feel the bizarre motion going on inside me. He jerked his hand away in disgust. My heart was hurt of course, but I was having such a good time as a prospective mother that it really didn't matter.

It didn't take long for Harvey to start shoving and hitting on me. He liked to draw back his fist and watch me flinch or duck, then he laughed and called me a stupid, whore. It didn't take much to fire off a fight. I refused to let him take the car to go frolicking. First of all, it was *my* car. Secondly, I may need it. Third, and most importantly, I didn't want him to wreck it. We had no insurance or money in our pockets. The last thing we needed was to have a baby and no vehicle. So he always managed to ride off with some of his friends, often a carload of guys *and* girls. I quickly grew to despise the partying scene. It took money, time, and energy that were desperately needed elsewhere, but he couldn't or *wouldn't* see that.

Late one night we were struggling in the snow over the car keys. I was eight months pregnant. With ignorant malice he shouted, "Fine! Neither one of us will have the car!" and threw the keys high into the dark sky and far into the woods behind our trailer. I focused my eyes on the keys and followed them to where they should have landed. I didn't care how pathetic or unattractive I looked. I *had* to find those keys. I took off running, tripping in the high snowdrifts and over unseen obstacles on the ground. I fell to my face several times as I kept my eyes focused on the spot where the keys must have landed. Harvey laughed like I was the dumbest, fumbling idiot he had ever seen. Sure enough, there they were, plopped down on the ground, right at the bottom of a tiny tunnel they drilled through the snow while plummeting to the cold earth! I was outside without a coat and needed to get dry and warm. Harvey had made his way to a chair in the living room by the time I got inside. The fight resumed. I was standing in front of him shivering, crying, and wishing he would leave (he often walked to find a party). The screaming match went on and on until he bent his head downward and propelled himself up out of the stuffed armchair like a bullet. With his stoned, dilated pupils glaring from under his forehead, he took purposeful aim and butted me in the belly with his head like a ram without a conscience. I screamed and grabbed my bulging belly. One of his friends had been standing by watching the entire time, hoping he would also get a ride to the nearest keg party. He pulled Harvey away from me and yelled, "Hey! Let's get outta' here!" and they did.

Chapter Ten

The baby was due the end of January, but like her mother, she got too curious for her own good. On December 30th, around 2:00 in the afternoon, my amniotic fluid started leaking. I was immediately admitted to the delivery room, and my labor was induced. That night passed, and into the next day, they discovered the baby's heart was getting weak from the hard, yet unsuccessful labor. It was New Year's Eve, and Harvey had party plans that he wasn't going to have interrupted, no matter what. All the family had gathered in the waiting room by dusk . . . everybody except Harvey. I had a device strapped around my belly that monitored the baby's heartbeat and the labor pains concurrently. We were both growing weaker and facing death. My cervix needed to open to ten centimeters, but after thirty hours of labor, it had opened to a mere four centimeters, not nearly enough to allow the baby to pass through. The baby's little heart finally gave up and stopped, announcing she had done enough and wanted to quit. I had felt the same way so many times in my life, but I was sure, since I had, she could also find the strength to live. I felt my own life slipping away as well. With mixed emotions, I whispered in God's ear and asked Him to please help us survive. The doctors and nurses scurried around trying hard to not panic. They had watched the two of us fight valiantly, while the expectant father staggered in and out of the hospital, visiting all the parties in town, each time more inebriated than his last visit. Despite our weariness, the medical experts weren't ready to give up. Miraculously, surprising some in the room, the baby's heart restarted and continued pumping its life-giving commodity. A surgeon was called in as they began preparing me for a cesarean section. Moments before I was about to be whisked from the room, another hard contraction, again, caused the baby's heart to stop. Time lapsed longer than during the previous episode. We stared at the monitor, praying for a little beep and a sharp peak to give us hope. Just a few minutes and they could have her out, if only she could hang on. The peak wasn't sharp, but it did appear, and off we went, nurses running while pushing my bed and hanging on to IV's and other apparatuses.

At 12:01 A.M., 2 January 1982, Jessica Lou made her dramatic debut. Wow, she was a gorgeous baby! She had a beautiful complexion and a head full of black, curly hair. A tiny thing she was, only four pounds, eleven ounces. Since the amniotic fluid sac never actually broke and labor carried on an extended amount of time, there was a threat of a serious infection entering the sac and affecting the baby. After birth the doctor examined the fluid remaining in her eyes, nose, ears, etc. He told me the fluid within her outer ear had already developed an infection, just a little longer in the womb, and she would have likely been deaf. Premature babies are often jaundice, therefore I wasn't extremely alarmed at her yellow skin. She also had a problem with her lungs. I'm ashamed to say I continued smoking cigarettes during the pregnancy, which greatly hindered the development of her lungs, specifically the tiny bronchioles. Breathing was difficult for her. I watched with a broken heart as her little body heaved, straining every moment to accomplish a sufficient intake of air. She struggled through that trial and came through without any lasting damage or symptoms.

While I was still under sedation, the nurses asked Harvey what we were going to name the baby. We hadn't agreed on the name. I wanted to call her Keda Lou, he wanted to name her after Jessie Colton, a female singer that traveled a lot with Willie Nelson. I hadn't thought of the matter, until the first time they brought her crib into my room for her feeding. There on the name tag was Jessica Lou Kissick. I wasn't really upset, it *was* a cute name. Believe it or not, in the bed next to me was a lady whose last name was Horse. She had a boy, and she and her husband named him Wild. I mentally acknowledged how things could be worse. Years later Jessica told me she thought Keda sounded like a dog's name and was glad it wasn't hers . . . God always has a good plan!

Jessica was the first baby of the year born in that particular hospital. We won some neat prizes, and she and I got our picture on the front page of the local newspaper. It took me a while to get the hang of motherhood. They taught me how to bathe her and change her diaper at the hospital (whew!). I wanted to breast feed her and that was sure an adventure! I was nervous about all the typical first-mother stuff . . . the umbilical cord, her bright green poop, SIDS.

I loved my new daughter more than
anything I had ever known.

Harvey was still in school but continued partying. I have to say he *did* love his cute, new, little baby. He was proud of her and just as I was, in awe of the miracle. But it wasn't enough to make him settle down and try to take care of his family. His dad gave him a school bus that had been painted blue. Harvey was talented at constructing and repairing things, especially motors and electrical items. He decided to strip the inside of the bus and make it into a camper. That sounded fine to me. It kept him busy, and it gave him a place to go drink and smoke that was out of the house, yet still at home. I also thought a camper was a fun idea, but it turned into a trick against me. By late that fall, Harvey quit school. That meant we had to move out of the university housing, and guess what? Into the bus we went! He had rigged up a barrel on its side for heat. It had two beds in the back, a shower, toilet, sink, electrical outlets, table, and couch, and a rail in front of the heat stove to keep Jessica from getting burnt.

The wood stove had a flue that went straight out the top of the bus. It puffed away as we trucked down the road, traveling from one friend's house to another. We plugged into their electricity and hung out for a few weeks, until we wore out our welcome. Finally we decided to park our bus on the land Dad had given us. There was no water or electricity (the electric company wouldn't run electricity very far from the main line for a nonpermanent residence), but I felt at peace there. Besides, I didn't see I had too many other options.

We spent a hard winter in that bus on our undeveloped property, nearly a mile from the highway, and I was sure glad when summer finally came. Harvey had picked up odd jobs here and there, as well as still selling drugs, but any extra money he got was spent on beer or liquor and more drugs. Most of his friends had been *my* friends at one time, and out of respect or discomfort, they rarely came around or tried to party at our place. Several of our old friends had married and had children or obtained good jobs and turned into social drinkers, but Harvey just couldn't let go of his old ways. "Party till 'ya puke!" was his motto. We cooked on an open fire or ate mostly cold foods. Jessica was growing out of baby food, and many times she ate canned green beans or carrots straight from the can. We sometimes showered in the rain or carried water from the pond, also on our property, for sponge baths. Harvey built a pump that was powered from the truck battery (He did finally demolish the car and *somehow* bought an old truck). He hung a garden hose over the rail of the truck and water dumped out in one weak stream. We had a large, barrel-shaped cooler that we filled with water and placed Jessica inside for her bath. She loved it; I suppose she didn't know there was any other way to bathe.

Bathtime!

The bank foreclosed on Dad and all his property went up for public auction. I decided to go to the auction, even though I really didn't want to experience the sadness of seeing him lose his lifetime of work, hopes, and dreams. One of the buildings for sale was a forty-by-seventy foot metal building with a concrete floor and an overhang which covered the front doors to create a nice, huge porch. With it was a large garage with sliding doors, all situated on an acre of land and lumped together by the auctioneer. I stood in the small crowd as the bidding began. It stalled at six thousand dollars! I was sure the bank would easily attach to the title and loan six thousand dollars for a piece of property like that. I was shaking out of my skin when I shouted, "Sixty-five hundred!" Faces looked at me with humored surprise, nobody bid against me, and it was mine.

I was surprised that Harvey was pleased. The bank gladly loaned us the money with his brother as a co-signer. The building was divided into two large rooms, it had no running water, but electricity. After two years in the school bus, it was sold and we moved into the metal building. I hung up old curtains and blankets on strung up wires for support. I divided the front room into a home: two bedrooms, living room, kitchen, and a bathroom. We placed an old toilet seat and lid on top of a bucket and used it for our toilet. When the bucket got fairly full, I carried it to the woods and dumped it out. There was a small stream that ran next to the property, and that provided the water for bathing. Harvey was happy to have a garage in which to tinker with all his junk cars and such. Sometimes he actually made some honest money out there.

I dread telling this part, but you deserve to know. I decided I wanted to try to put together a modeling portfolio and pursue some modeling jobs either locally or in Lexington. I met a man who was an instructor in the photography department at the university. He raved about the value of my beauty and claimed to have important connections in this field and wanted to help me. We got together for a few photo shoots, and he produced several proof sheets for me . . . all this at the expense of the university. I regret it horribly, but he eventually convinced me to do some nude modeling. At the time it didn't touch my conscience . . . I hardly had one . . . honestly . . . I felt beautiful. I always posed alone and usually in shadowed, misty atmospheres. Once he described a pose he was looking for . . . a hustler, erotic-type position. I hit it perfectly while he snapped away with his camera and cheered my performance. I felt vexed . . . undone . . . I quickly moved to another pose . . . and never produced that type of look again. Harvey was in favor of the whole thing, or so he said at the time. A few years later he admitted he hated it and resented me for doing it . . . I don't blame him.

As I grew more independent, the physical abuse intensified. Harvey carried a gun, and on several occasions he threatened me with it or shot at me or in the air. Most times he intended to miss, but once he took dead aim right at me as I was running away with Jessica in my arms. His drunkenness caused him to miss. Another time, while fleeing for my life *again*, I tossed Jessica into her baby seat in the car and tried to speed away to safety. Harvey chased us and beat out the windshield with a club, spraying glass all over Jessica and me. His favorite form of torture was holding me down on the wood stove. He thrilled at the sight of my horrified face as he held it inches from red-hot, scalding metal. My back was burned several times, but never anything that left permanent scars. He was *always* very careful to not leave evidence . . . the only thing he was afraid of was the law.

I worked as a waitress for several years while Harvey took care of Jessica. I was satisfied with the arrangement, and he seemed to handle it fairly well also. I didn't approve of him partying with Jessica, but I knew he loved her, and I had to believe he would keep her protected. Now understand, wild parties don't usually *start out* wild . . . many times they begin as peaceful and quite therapeutic. A lot of times several friends just happen to stop in, burn a "doobie," split a case of beer, and relax together. Before one knows it, the house or yard is full of partiers, on all sorts of highs and starting to rumble. That posed a problem for little children, especially at a stranger's home. (It wasn't unusual for several small children to be running around at the parties.)

Jessica was a sharp little kid. (Really! She truly was.) She knew when Harvey was getting too high and unaware of her. I guess you can tip your hat to Harvey for this . . . when it got late and she got sleepy, Harvey took off his black, leather, biker jacket and found a safe corner to hide it. He instructed Jessica to "guard" his most favored possession from being stolen, by lying on the jacket and sleeping there until he came back for it. It was a routine they established and followed night after night. In her little heart, I think she knew Daddy would come back for his black, leather jacket, even if he forgot *her*.

Chapter Eleven

Incredibly I became pregnant again. Harvey and I had long grown apart and rarely met in bed. I was sure he was having relations with several different women and was also sure he had fathered another child with one of his partying girlfriends. Because of all these factors, I am convinced that God ordained that pregnancy.

Perhaps one child was sporting to Harvey, he played along and generally tolerated the demands, but he didn't cope well with the prospects of another baby. I was also in crisis. I asked myself over and over, "How could you let this happen? How will you care for another child? What are you going to do?" The questions tumbled endlessly through my mind. I honestly wasn't sure I had the strength or love to stretch far enough to cover this little baby.

Abortion absolutely *never* entered my mind, with either of my children, neither did adoption, or any other alternative besides having the baby and facing the music. Somehow I would make it through.

The fighting was getting dangerous. Harvey even chased me with an ax and swung at my advanced pregnant belly. Only my quick feet kept the baby and me alive. He was beating me worse everyday, using his fist and punching me in the belly. Unable to work, I stayed home with Jessica, while each evening, he prepared to go out and find a party. Many times he started a fight before he left and told me he would be back to kill me, often describing how he would do it and how much he was going to enjoy it. Sometime around 3:00 or 5:00 A.M. he would come staggering through the door. I spent many sleepless nights,

lying awake, waiting in fear for him to return. I listened carefully, as he opened the door and walked through the room to
his bed. I could tell by the sound of his steps whether he was
going to start a fight or simply pass out.

Dad and Wanda were having problems too. Wanda had a
good job as a secretary at the university, but Dad believed she
was fooling around with some guy in the office. I didn't see
them much, except when he came asking for money. He would
get upset and belittle me when I didn't have any to give him.

Mom was single and working hard. She was a lot of support during this time. Many times I fled to her home seeking
refuge. Sometimes she gave me money or bought me new
clothes to wear. One time she bought Jessica and me each a
new Easter dress and hat, of course to wear to church with her.
And that was the most valuable gift my Mother ever gave
me . . . a sense of spirituality. Of all the things she may have
taken *or withheld* from me, her faith in God instilled in me
superseded them all. She called on the phone inviting us to
church every week. I normally made excuses or simply refused
to go, but sometimes I felt I owed it to her to be there.

Now remember this is a "holiness church." They want you
kneeling at the altar sobbing away for your wretched wickedness by the end of the service, and you're not likely to get away
until you do. It took some heavy-duty, stubborn indifference to
get out of there without "getting saved." That usually wasn't a
problem for me; but there I was, five months pregnant with a
2½-year-old, driving a beat-up old junker, and looking like a
trampled flower. The preacher, Brother Gary Henson, poured
out his heart while looking right at me. I can't remember the
sermon, just the plea for repentance.

Mom left the service early that day to go to work. The
congregation had been dismissed and people were filing out
the door. I was collecting my child and our belongings (Harvey
almost never went to church) when my Aunt Kay stopped to
give me a hug. It made me cry. "You need to pray," she said
sweetly. I nodded my head, chuckled, and said "Yea, I *sure* do."
I didn't mean I *wanted* to pray, just that I was fully aware that
my life was in shambles . . . my little girl and soon-to–arrive

child deserved more than they were getting . . . things were downright terrible and I had no hope . . . but I *still* didn't *want* to pray! Aunt Kay motioned for some others to join her, "Connie wants to pray," she told them.

Everybody got so excited, I hated to let them down, so up to the altar they led me. Aunt Madge took charge of baby-sitting Jessica. Helen Patton took the right side, Aunt Kay, the left. Uncle Harold sat on the front pew smiling and hiding an occasional tear. I already had on my coat when I was pulled to the front. They didn't dare distract me by trying to remove it, so I knelt at the altar with it on. I knew how it was done and might have gotten through the scene without anything *really* happening, if only the Holy Spirit had stayed out of it. But He didn't (Thanks, Lord). Several others were gathered around and praying loudly for the forgiveness of my sins and courage to live for Christ. I listened to them more than I prayed for myself. I cried a lot just because I needed a good cry, not necessarily because I was sorry for my sins. They prayed for a long time, perhaps an hour, and then each one started giving me advice on how to be a Christian, and to not expect too much out of myself at first. "It's a growing process," they said. "Just trust the Lord; take it one step at a time; forgive your-self . . ." Sweat and tears were running down the side of my face; Helen Patton laughed and squeezed me as she said with a country accent, "You've been diggin', Honey, you've been diggin'."

Then somewhere in all of that, it seemed the Holy Spirit whispered softly, simply, and only one time . . . something to the effect of, "How about it? Do you want to live for Me?" I sat back and pondered the thought. I didn't think I could really do it. I refused to be an unscrupulous hypocrite. It took mighty guts, like doing something heroic, to say, "Yes," in my heart. So after the praying was done, as we sat on the closest pew to relax and rejoice, I made the decision to live for the Lord Jesus Christ, the Son of God, the One who died a horrible death on the cross at Calvary for my sins. I didn't cry, laugh, or make any outward sign of my conversion. It was simply a decision, a stamp of ownership proudly and decisively pounded with one astonishing move of the hand of God. I knew it wouldn't be easy (it wasn't), and I might make a lot of mistakes (I *did)*. It might even cost my life (it would, so to speak). My innate, stubborn disposition would not make it happen, but the love, forgiveness, and protection of God . . . would.

Chapter Twelve

I dreaded leaving the church that day I accepted Jesus into my heart. As I sat there on the front pew, I turned and looked at the door several times while mustering the nerve to go home. My family and friends sat with me in the sanctuary, sensing my fear and lack of confidence. Jessica and I finally left and went to visit my Grandmother who was very ill. Mamaw Griffey was in bed and trying to eat some grapes. I lay down beside her, held the plate, and slowly fed her one grape at a time. She had no strength to talk but forced herself to ask about "Jessi*cut*" (her pet name for her). "She's fine," I said. I told her a funny thing Jessica had done that week, and she smiled but couldn't respond with any more animation. After a few moments of silence, I said, "I got saved today, Mamaw." It seemed I felt her heart skip a beat. Her tired, old body twitched with enthusiasm as her hoarse voice crackled sweet words of simple confirmation, "Good, Connie Lou." It was only a few short weeks later that Mamaw Griffey passed away.

After our visit, we headed home. I was relieved Harvey was home. I wanted to tell him right away before I lost my courage. I overestimated his awareness of spiritual things. It turned out he didn't know what it meant to get saved, accept Jesus, or become a Christian. He did, however, understand when I said I wouldn't be swearing, drinking, or smoking dope anymore. It didn't matter to him. He said, "Whatever turns you on," and left it at that. I immediately tried to love him more and not be quarrelsome. Later that evening Jessica and I readied ourselves to return to church for the night service, and that *was* a problem. Harvey had party plans, which meant *he* wanted the car.

That was the first of many dilemmas I would encounter while trying to weigh my Christian obedience against the responsibilities of being a submissive wife. Jessica and I made it to church that night, had a great time, and returned to a house full of marijuana smoke and stoned bodies. I tried to be good. I really did. Yet after much coaxing and chiding, I fell to their offer and smoked a joint with them. I felt conviction the entire time, even while on a slight buzz. As uncomfortable as it was, I marveled at the strangeness of feeling God's voice and presence about me. I was sad to have flopped as a Christian so soon, but I just knew that wasn't the end of it. My upbringing had taught me about grace, mercy, and endless forgiveness, but I felt more than the "teaching." I heard it in my heart, I saw it in my unusual tears.

Since the attacks from Randall C., I had been sleeping with a Bible under my pillow. It was a defense that became a crutch. Regardless of its theological invalidity or implications, it worked. If I spent the night at someone else's house and lay down without first finding a Bible to place under my pillow, I would startle at the edge of sleep. Always awakening with a jolt to find there wasn't really a man standing beside my bed or an ugly face, just inches from my own. I decided to start reading the Bible. My reasoning was elementary . . . better to have the Bible *in* my head instead of *under* my head. The Word of God intrigued me . . . it became as an engrossing novel to me. There was now a precious voice in my heart that flowed along with each passage . . . touching my spirit with realness. Inexplicable depth awakened inside me as never before, a realization that grew each session I spent reading the Bible.

Brenda Henson was the pastor's wife, as well as a full-time nurse and mother of three little boys. She was young, unattractive and "real." Brother Henson, her husband, was young and nervous. A new convert is an exciting project for ambitious, new ministers. Sometimes they study, pray, and work for years before they have the thrill of seeing the countenance change on a newborn Christian. It was fortunate for me, they took me under their wings. Brenda convinced me to start helping her in Junior Church. If new Christians are diamonds in the rough, then I should have been called freshly mined coal, but there I was the next Sunday morning ready to serve, humble as it was. Brenda kept close tabs on me and gave me assignments to complete for church, like typing the bulletin or preparing the craft item for next Sunday's lesson. Brother Henson was afraid of Harvey and couldn't reach out to me. That was okay. I understood.

As I grew in the knowledge of Christ, my second child grew in my small belly. I had quit smoking cigarettes right after getting saved, and the baby's growth took off! I had no idea how much a fetus could stretch. She stretched her little legs and poked her foot in my side to where I could actually count her tiny toes through my skin! Without the tobacco, I felt more alive and had more coping power. Jessica and I prepared the baby's little bed and clothes with wide-eyed anticipation and grandeur. She had no idea we were poor and our surroundings were miserable. We pretended to be fairy princesses, playing house in a castle and looking forward to seeing the newborn royalty. The church had a diaper party for me, and I received over forty large packages of disposable diapers, an act of kindness that got Harvey's attention, but not enough to change him.

It was a calm night, no drinking or fighting, when I started experiencing labor pains. I tried to talk myself out of it, until they were five minutes apart and my stomach hardened with each contraction. So in the middle of the night I drove myself to the hospital, asking Harvey to stay with Jessica. Our car at that time was a worn out "boat" with a huge motor that guzzled the gasoline. We added to the tank whatever we could afford, two dollars or maybe five dollars worth of gasoline at a time. Without an alternate plan and five miles from the hospital, I ran out of gas. I walked to a friend's house, about a half mile, and banged on their bedroom window to awaken them. I finally arrived at the hospital in full labor.

After an examination, they told me my water hadn't broken, and the baby wasn't in danger yet. If she were born now though, she wouldn't be likely to survive. They put me in the delivery room and hooked me up to IV's and the same monitors used with Jessica. I was anxious for the baby to come but I knew it was too soon, way too soon; so I started to pray. This time I knew Who I was talking to and despite my failures, He was listening and caring.

The hours passed as the IV dripped continuously into my veins. With each drop the baby calmed, and for the time being, submitted to the ultimate plan. The labor ceased by evening, and I was kept for observation. The next day I called Harvey to come get me.

They gave me a drug to take for the remainder of the pregnancy, hopefully eight more weeks, and gave me strict instructions to stay in bed twenty-four hours a day. Harvey let me down quite a bit during that time, but he did help out some. Jessica wasn't fed very well, but she was tough and took care of herself, as well as helped me. I think the medication was called yutopar, and vicious stuff it was! It made me nervous and tremble relentlessly. Several times Harvey held me safely in bed while I convulsed uncontrollably. It was all normal, and I had to endure it, if there was any hope of saving the baby. Despite our tedious efforts, the baby would not remain in her safe environment. Four weeks later, in the heat of a humid, Appalachian summer, my labor began again.

Back in the hospital, Harvey made a visit and was cordial with my church friends. The doctor wasn't convinced the baby was close enough to full term to survive outside the womb. They successfully stopped the labor with an IV and medication, but decided to arrange the C-section sooner than planned. There was a fear that too much stress was being placed on the fetus and she wouldn't live through another episode of hard labor. They promised me if the baby and I could make it just one more week, they would go ahead with the delivery. They set the date for surgery on the following Friday at 9:00 A.M. I was to check into the hospital at 1:00 P.M. the previous day. That was a strange way to have a baby, but I certainly wasn't complaining. All I had to do was keep her safely inside until then.

Harvey and Jessica escorted me to the hospital admissions office and waited anxiously for the paper work to be completed.

They gave me an identification bracelet and called for the mandatory wheelchair. The nurse arrived to carry me to my room and informed us Jessica wouldn't be allowed to accompany me upstairs to my room. I had to part with her right there in the waiting room, leaving her in Harvey's arms, looking worried and disappointed. Later that night Harvey's mother watched Jessica while he came to visit me. He was sober, and we had a short, but nice visit. I was relaxed and confident things were going to be all right at home as well as in the hospital.

Morning came and the surgeon was delayed. My surgery was put off for several hours, which meant the family that had gathered also had to wait. They hung in there, and I was finally taken in to the operating room. I had been through the procedure once before and was cooperative and cheery. I sat up and folded over like a frog while they administered the spinal tap. One of the nurses announced with frustration that the nurses downstairs hadn't inserted my catheter. There were two parts of a Caesarean-section birth that I dreaded: the catheter and the pressing they do on the uterus (near the incision) for several days following the surgery to remove blood clots. I felt it was an answer to prayer that I was already numb when the catheter was inserted.

One of the assistants asked if he could begin, and the masked surgeon nodded a baffled, "Yes." They strapped my arms down and began to cut open my tummy with a tool that sounded like a miniature skill saw. I was fully awake and alert as I watched the assistant start below my bellybutton, cutting strategically straight up and over my rounded abdomen. The sound of muscles pulling apart was more than I could handle. My already-normally-low blood pressure dropped to a dangerously lower level. An alarmed voice warned the surgeon. He immediately cited some orders that made no sense to me. The table started lifting hydraulically from my feet, tilting me swiftly into a near-up-side-down position. (I learned later the reason for this was to lower my head, in order to speed the effects of the spinal tap, and alleviate the intensity of the moment.) I remained that way for several minutes, vomiting into a pan

held next to my face, waiting out the crisis. Everyone stopped
. . . staring at the beeping, telling machines . . . waiting . . .
waiting . . . more words I didn't understand . . . "All clear!"
someone shouted.

The table was lowered and their work resumed with a
little more adrenaline. I couldn't control the panic that hit me.
I started crying and begging to be loosened from the straps. A
nurse stood at my head, leaning directly over the top and back
of my shivering body and looking into my eyes. "You'll be all
right, Honey. You must stay calm," she tried. I thrashed my
body, demanding without consideration to be freed. Over and
over, each one around the table, perhaps eight or twelve assistants, nurses, etc., said, "We can't undo the straps. Please, you
must lie still."

"Just bend my legs. If you'll just bend my legs, I think I'll
be okay," I pleaded with a little more awareness in my voice.
They finally consented, unstrapped my ankles, and bent my
legs carefully at the knees.

In the meantime, the surgeon had been working his way
through several layers of tissue and carefully making his way to
the baby. I quieted the moment they bent my knees, and everyone relaxed and began to enjoy the show. This was the moment for which they had invested their lives. Somewhere, perhaps as children, these miracle workers made a career choice,
perhaps even huge sacrifices, that would allow them to usher
life into existence . . . the privilege of assisting God as His hands
made a miracle. They hushed and huddled around the table as
the surgeon approached the fetus. I felt pressure but no pain.
I heard squishing sounds as his arms moved in, out, up, around.
He was bent over me like a virtuoso, concert pianist performing
a passionate arrangement that few truly appreciate. There was
a sheet propped up between my face and the action below.
They saw her first. "It's a girl!" Several shouted simultaneously.
She was lifted high enough for me to see her, covered in blood,
skin purplish-black-blue, body wrinkled, and very, very tiny. A
nurse carried her away . . . she didn't cry. I thought that was
odd; Jessica was crying before they lifted her from within my
belly . . . I got scared. Busy work resumed in the room. They

weren't really worried, just working seriously. "Is she okay?" I asked timidly, fearful of the answer. No response. I anxiously waited, not wanting to interrupt their train of thought. It was a squeak at first, then a whimper, and finally, she gained momentum and cried out with arioso volume! I instantly broke into sobs and secretly thanked God. A nurse cleaned up her little body, wrapped her in a blanket, put a funny hat on her head, and brought her to me. She gently placed the baby's face against my cheek and let us linger there as long as possible. It was a beautiful, perfect thing for that blessed nurse to do. I will remember the moment forever.

She weighed a whopping five pounds, one ounce. Her black hair was thick and curly. She was able and ready to nurse right away, so the family quickly trailed through my room and left Harvey and me to stare in awe at our baby. I don't remember much after that. I was ready to sleep.

We agreed on the name Lacy Dawn. It suited her too. Her tender, frail body was soft, delicate, and lovely. She had a slight case of jaundice, but other than that there seemed to be no other problems. I suppose like all mothers, I counted her toes and fingers and examined every pimple on her face. I even checked the crown in her hair . . . it was perfect! She would be glad as a teenager to have a normal hairline and crown. I cautiously treated her sore navel and waited for the crusted, black top to detach itself and fall away.

It was prearranged for Jessica to stay with Harvey's elderly mother during the operation. She wasn't able to go out of the house for long, so she agreed to keep Jessica and then visit the baby after we got home. Harvey was suppose to pick up Jessica after he left the hospital . . . but he didn't.

Chapter Thirteen

Lacy and I had been in the hospital three days when a nurse came into my room and told me I had a phone call at the nurses' station. (The extra fee for a bedside phone prevented me from requesting one.) I hobbled my way down the hall and was surprised to hear my mother-in-law on the other end of the line. She sounded feeble and apologetic. "When is Harvey coming to get Jessica?" she asked after the initial inquiries. I was shocked. She hadn't seen Harvey since he dropped off Jessica before the surgery. He hadn't been at the hospital visiting Lacy and me either. That hadn't upset me since I had assumed he was home with Jessica, and that was where I preferred he be. But instead, his mother was tiring of chasing a 2-year-old, needed a break, and Harvey was no where to be found. It wasn't unusual for Harvey to disappear for several days, but I didn't expect him to do this now! I hung up the phone and tried calling places I thought he might be, with no luck. Exhausted, I gave up and went back to my hospital bed. Harvey showed up that evening, with his motorcycle helmet under his arm, looking strung-out and hung over. I don't remember his explanation, or if he attempted to give me one. He did go pick up Jessica, and a few days later, he came to pick up Lacy and me from the hospital.

We still didn't have running water in our home. Harvey had found a cheap water tank and cobbled it to run cold water into the bathroom and kitchen sink. We had a *real* toilet, which had to be flushed with a bucket of water (usually once every few days), that ran into a hole dug just behind the building. I couldn't depend on Harvey to be around when the water tank emptied, so I used the water sparingly since he was the one that had to haul the tank to town, fill it, and reconnect it back at home.

The incision on my stomach was nearly eight inches long and required special care, just as Lacy's little body did. It was typically hot and muggy. The flies swarmed freely through our opened doors. When the baby slept, I placed a fan directly in front of her and draped an old sheer curtain over her to keep the flies off. God protected us from infections and sickness that easily could have originated in such foul conditions.

It was a special treat to take the little girls to my mother's now old and used trailer house to do laundry. We turned on the air conditioner and bathed in luxury! Mom disliked my situation and often made me feel disgraced to need her help. She was working long hours and trying to cope with some struggles of her own. Despite the strain, she encouraged me in the ways of the Lord and tried to help as much as possible. Sometimes she gave Harvey and me money to pay the electric bill or took the girls and I out to eat after church. I was growing up and learning to forgive . . . the healing between us was beginning.

Lacy brought renewed hope, joy, and strength into all our tattered hearts.

I was in church "every time the doors were open." Sometimes I had to call for a ride, but I was determined to be there. I sat on the edge of the pew, following every sermon with keen interest. I wanted nothing to slip by me. My hunger for an understanding of God's teaching was a consuming, driving force. Nearly every service I went to the altar to pray, either for repentance for the weeks' sins or for courage, strength . . . you name it . . . I needed it! The church members were dear, old saints that had known me since birth. They took my success as a Christian as their personal assignment from God, whom they loved dearly. That love was transferred to me as they prayed and cried with me, counseled me, and cared for my children. Many times I would be the last to leave the church, staying late to ask Bro. Henson some important scriptural question, mostly not wanting to leave the sweet atmosphere and dreading the scene I might face at home. I once was troubled about tithing. I had no income of my own. At the time, the only income we had as a family was Harvey's profit from selling drugs. After a lengthy discussion, I was relieved when Bro. Henson advised me not to worry about trying to tithe Harvey's drug money.

I volunteered to direct the summer Vacation Bible School program. I had lots of enthusiasm and ideas but was short on cash. I knew I wouldn't be able to afford the gas to get to church every night for a week. I prayed and the next week, without a hint to Mom, she handed me ten dollars for gas, just enough to do the job!

*   *   *   *   *

Harvey and I continued to grow apart. I tried to hide the fighting from the girls, but it was becoming more difficult. Sometimes he would involve Jessica and try to turn her against me. He was more aggressive toward them and beginning to be abusive in discipline. One time he literally threw Jessica out the door onto the graveled driveway. When she lifted her little face, a rock protruded from her forehead and blood was gushing from the wound. Many times I fled for our lives, dragging the children along like a cartoon, only to return after his tearful pleas and promises to change. I always hoped *this time* would be different, and he *really would* change. Sometimes to appease me after a terrible argument or fight, he would accompany us to church. Once he went to the altar and claimed to "get saved" after seeing lightening bolts. I think it was a sincere experience, but it didn't last for more than a few days. I believe Harvey deeply felt his inadequacy as a husband and father. I also think he had a touch of genius that was never fostered or channeled correctly. Whatever his problems were, they drove him to near madness, and the only solace he trusted was artificial, expensive, and deadly to himself and his family.

*   *   *   *   *

Unexpectedly, a man approached us wanting to buy our building/home and land. He had a 20-year-old trailer house he wanted to trade for it, in addition to some "boot" money. I jumped at the chance to have a *real* shelter! We still owned the land Dad gave us for a wedding present. It was a beautiful, wooded lot that would easily provide space for the trailer, but it was nearly a half-mile to the nearest water tap and electric pole. As part of the transaction, the buyer agreed to use his own bulldozer to clear a spot for the trailer and create a makeshift driveway. We used the money obtained in the trade to pay the movers to transport the mobile home to its new location and to start building Harvey another garage in which to work. He bought lumber, nails, and beer. He invited his friends, and they constructed a shell of a garage that would have sufficed, but we ran out of money before it was roofed. It was never completed and stood as another shameful reminder of poor planning and lack of resolve.

After the trailer was in place, Harvey was given an old truck bed, which he decided would make a nice room addition to the trailer. I felt sick as I watched him tear out one whole wall in the living room and butt the truck bed up next to the jagged wall. He patched up the edges and was successful in keeping out the ensuing icy rain and snow. The barrel stove was situated in the truck bed, so it quickly became the wood room and an eye sore. But it kept the trailer warm, and it was safely away from the little girls that were now running merrily through the house. Harvey looked like a wild heretic as he sawed down trees and brought in firewood. Keeping a fire going all winter is a fairly big task and was a chore that eventually became my responsibility. I never tried to run the chainsaw. Fortunately, Harvey always had logs cut for me, but a lot of times he would quit before the wood was split into burnable wedges. A round log is nice to stoke the fire with at night before retiring but puts off little heat and serves poorly as daytime, comfortable warmth. I tried to use the maul to split the logs, but my arms just didn't have enough thrust. I tried wrestling a whole log through the opening in the end of the barrel, praying it would burn hot enough to keep the trailer warm. Sometimes the girls and I would sit beside the stove with a blanket around us as I read them stories and played quiet, sit-down games. I think that was the first time God spoke clearly to my heart. As I struggled with those logs, often burning and scraping my hands, I breathed the same insult over and over, "I hate you, Harvey Kissick. I hate you . . ." It gave me strength to keep going and made me feel superior to the circumstances he had put us in. The Lord was straight with me (an attribute of our relationship I would grow to trust and appreciate) as He told me not to hate. He said, "There is strength in hate; watch out for it!" It is one of the many lessons I have learned that I don't want to repeat.

We had an old car we called the "Blue Bug," that wouldn't start until the driver raised up off the seat and pumped the accelerator as the starter tried to turn over the groggy motor. It sounds absurd, I know, but I was told there was a wire to the starter strung under the seat. When weight was in the seat, the wire shorted out. "Blue Bug" got us in and out of the woods that winter, unless the snow or mud was too deep. There was a long, steep hill to climb to get to our property. It was unprotected by barriers on either side. Sliding over the edge, barring a miracle, would be tragic. Sometimes as I slid down the ungraveled road, I would have to throw the transmission in reverse and floor the gas pedal, giving myself enough backward pull to avoid going over the edge. Going up wasn't usually as hazardous as long as I backed up as far as I could on the opposite, mountainous hill, revved the engine, and took off with enough speed to clear the peak of the opposing hill. Country folks would call it "Getting a good running start!" If it bogged out before reaching the top, I would leave it parked there in the sticky mud, walk home, and back the vehicle down the hill later when the road was drier.

One night the girls and I went to church. Someone had given me a pair of gray, suede boots that I wore with a "yard sale" pink-and-gray-checked skirt. I was proud of my boots and felt pretty in them. That night coming home, our Bug wouldn't climb the hill. I had to get out and walk the rest of the way home. As I opened the door and stepped into mud over my ankles, I knew my boots were ruined. Jessica said, "Oh, Mommy, your boots!" I took her hand and carried Lacy, our Bibles, and bags through the dark, as I made excuses to comfort my observant, compassionate daughter. "I really didn't like them that much . . . they hurt my feet," I said.

It was that terrible winter that I realized my children had to have a better home life. I enrolled in a government program that paid low-income participants a salary while they attended vocational school. I chose a cosmetology school in Morehead, nine miles away. The program would take nine months to complete, and then I hoped to establish my own income and be more secure. Dad, Wanda, and Anna lived just below us in the hollow, so they baby-sat quite a bit. Anna was big enough to watch the kids and enjoyed the company. Harvey was unreliable as a baby-sitter, so I rarely left them in his care. One day I was in a bind and had to leave them with Harvey, even though he complained and yelled about some previous plans he had made with his buddies. I returned that evening and didn't find them at home. I called every place I could imagine where he might have left them but could not locate them. I knew they weren't with Harvey because one of his friends told me he saw him and some others going to a party out of town. It was dark and getting late and I was starting to worry. Finally the neighbor down the road, people I didn't like or trust, called to ask when I was coming for the kids. I was outraged that he had left them with strangers and didn't leave me a note or any clue of how to find them. That was the beginning of our final separation.

Chapter Fourteen

Having the trailer house had given me new confidence. I had a home that would shelter my children and now an income of my own. Harvey stayed away from home for weeks at a time, only to show up with a stench, colorless skin, and peevish mood. He'd dig around in the kitchen and curse me for never having anything decent to eat. Then he would head for the shower, change clothes, play with the girls, tell them he loved them, and many times dash out again before dark. I made the mistake of telling them he had to go to work. I couldn't bear telling them their father would rather hang out with scummy addicts than with them. It was too harsh and unbelievable. I waited for a time that I thought Harvey would be gone for a while to make a move, hoping it wouldn't cause too much of an uproar until it was too late.

I made arrangements to have my trailer moved to a rented lot in Morehead. It had electricity, bottled gas for the furnace and kitchen appliances, running water, and a city sewer . . . all the conveniences I had lived without for four out of six years of marriage! My brother helped unblock the trailer and get it ready to move. It took two bulldozers to keep everything from sliding and crashing to the bottom of the long, muddy hill one pulling from the front, the other connected to the rear of the trailer, providing a safety hold with a thick, tense chain. The mud was deep as we tromped around in the freezing rain, but we got it down from what many would call a mountain and on to the highway headed toward town. Dad and Billy helped me block and level it. We found some old lumber, which Billy used to board up the hole left in the wall where the truck bed had been attached. I had saved enough money to turn on the utilities, and we had heat at the flip of a switch in a few weeks. The girls and I danced around the living room after bathing in our own tub and eating a nice, hot meal. It was great!

By the time Harvey caught up with us, we were already set up and enjoying the ease of day-to-day tasks. He liked the way I had things under control (after all, he didn't have to help do any of it), and he wanted to make amends. Don't groan too loudly. It's almost over, but not until after the next chapter, which tells of another mistake that I wish I could skip over and pretend didn't happen.

Chapter Fifteen

I was still driving over twenty miles to Garvin Ridge to church. Bro. Henson and Brenda felt their time was over there and a new preacher was brought in. I'll say his name was Bro. Bondage. He was an overweight blowhole that thought holiness meant never cutting hair or wearing pants or makeup. I tried to subscribe to his beliefs for a while. For two months I never wore anything that resembled pants or makeup.

Jessica insisted on taking my picture before I left
to attend the class graduation of a local modeling school.
I was honored to emcee the event.

During that time period, I graduated from Beauty School, a few months after the space shuttle "Challenger" exploded during lift off. I began working full-time in a salon close to our house. Harvey straightened up for a while and got a good job in Lexington, over one hundred miles away. We got a nice little truck and found a good baby-sitter. Things were running fairly smooth for a while. Then Harvey showed up where I worked in the middle of the day. I knew he was going to have some far-out story about why he wasn't at work, but I was impressed that he bothered to tell me anything at all. The story was he got fired for stealing oil, which he claimed he was going to put back.

Stealing was one of Harvey's many problems, but the one I found most disgusting was lying. He would lie for no reason. When the truth was more believable or less likely to provoke an argument, he would *still* make up a lie. I never understood why he did that, but it made me completely intolerable of liars. Few things (there *are* a few) on earth, do I despise equally or more than liars.

I later discovered the real reason Harvey was fired from that job in Lexington. He was assisting the front desk attendant in dealing drugs. This is how it worked. People came in the front door and, if all was clear, made their drug request and paid the clerk behind the counter, who then filled out a fake service order and gave it to Harvey. The drugs were taped under the toilet tank lid, so Harvey simply went to the restroom, retrieved the appropriate amount of drugs, then placed them under the floor mat of the buyer's car. All this was done right under nose of the manager and owners, at least for a while.

A new tire store was opening in the town where we lived. The manager recognized Harvey's talents and hired him right away. He was well paid, and working close to home resulted in extra money for spending. Harvey started partying again and staying out for days or weeks at a time. When he did come home, he was uninterested in the children and he always left early for work. I was sure he had a girlfriend.

I was working for a lady named Marty Reed. She owned a small beauty shop positioned in the enclosed back porch of her house. I could walk to work, and she didn't mind if my children had to come along. She often baby-sat her grandchildren and they quickly became friends with my girls, which helped keep all of them out of the way.

Marty and I had worked out an agreement that allowed me to open my own Reflexology office next to the shop. It was an interest I had pursued at my mother's coaxing and funding, after a Reflexologist finally cured an extended, peculiar illness of hers. The theory behind the practice is that there are distinct pressure points in the feet and hands that correspond to every part of the body. It is believed by some that massaging these points can promote and restore health to an afflicted body. I thought it was fascinating to watch it work, and I enjoyed helping people feel better.

Marty also had two tanning beds that stayed booked until late into the night. Marty's husband pastored a church in Ohio, which meant they were normally out of town by Friday evening, and the shop was left for me to manage. I tried hard to do a good job for her and gain her confidence.

One evening a handsome, 50-year-old, distinguished-looking man came in to get a quick haircut. He flirted with me the instant he stepped into the room where I was alone. Nobody had flirted with me in years, and he caught me off guard. I sat him in the styling chair and reclined the back for a shampoo as we began a genial conversation. He was Jack B., single, and in the heat of a campaign, vying for a high-ranking political office. Jack was curious about Reflexology and wondered if it would help him relax from his hectic and intense schedule. I didn't need to sales-pitch him; I had all the business I cared to handle. He offered to pay me well if I could manage to treat him in his home. I had visited several elderly people at home and ignorantly saw no problem with going to *his* home. We made an appointment for a treatment in the near future, he paid for his haircut, including a generous tip, and out the door he went. I thought nothing more of it.

Squeezing in a Reflexology house call was inconvenient and didn't interest me. But I had already made the appointment and decided to keep it. After arranging for a baby-sitter,

I gathered the supplies I'd need for a therapeutic foot massage. I packed a heated, vibrating footbath and special herbs and lotions. I also took along an electric massager that I used on each client's back at the conclusion of every treatment.

Jack lived in a nice suburb and had a lovely home with a deck that overlooked a pond and a secluded, wooded area. I arrived on time, and he was expecting me. He met me at the door, gave me a tour of the outside grounds, and then invited me in. I went to work setting up my equipment while he made small talk. In my office, clients sat in a quiet room soaking their feet while I tended to other customers in another room. It was a vital part of the treatment, not only for cleansing but to soften calloused skin and relax the muscles as well. I also had a custom-built, padded chiropractic table on which the client reclined while their feet rested in my lap and hands. I felt it was a reputable service, though now I question its integrity. In a person's home, I simply used two facing chairs, which is what I did at Jack's. I decided to not mention the back massage and prepared to make my exit. He handed me one-hundred dollars with ease (my quoted fee was twenty dollars) and asked if I would come back the next week. Wide eyed, I choked a flabbergasted, "Yes."

Jack decided he needed a tan since his appearance on television was becoming more frequent. He made appointments at Marty's shop and talked political niceties with the other waiting customers while I stayed busy cutting and styling hair. Jack made a point of treating me special, even in front of other people. It wasn't always as though he was flirting, just gracious and tender. He did, however, turn on the charm when we were alone. One night he came for a late tanning bed appointment. I was alone in the shop. He stood at the door of his tanning booth and slowly unbuttoned his shirt, exposing his tanned, hairy chest, while facing me standing ten feet away. I nervously tried to ignore the obvious. He was purposefully working me, breaking me down, drawing me in, seducing me . . . and a part of me was enjoying it.

For six months Jack and I carried on with each other like newlyweds. The pretense of therapy was done away with, and it became a full-blown affair. I hid my vehicle in his garage so the media wouldn't catch wind of the scandal. I lay in his bed and cried in his arms as I shared the abusive stories of my marriage. For him I suppose it was a release, a getaway, as well. We each had our reasons; we served a purpose for each other, and I don't resent him for anything more than what millions of others do every day . . . fall to sexual sin. Jack won the election in November, moved to Frankfort, the state capitol, and we lost touch.

*   *   *   *   *

It was hard getting to church. The long drive and the affair with Jack were all the reasons I needed to stay away. Marty, my boss, was a Pentecostal, which meant she believed everything a Christian believes, as well as the realness of the gifts of the Holy Spirit, most specifically (at the time) praying in tongues. I accompanied her to a local church several times and thoroughly enjoyed the dynamic worship . . . clapping, dancing, lifting hands, and shouting . . . it was a celebration of whom we are when born again and into the kingdom of God. I was accustomed to Bro. Bondage's tongue lashing every Sunday, hearing about my innate wickedness and inability to live a sinless life. Now those words are true enough, but I think God prefers to remind us of how wonderfully and fearfully we are created, how He loves us so much He gave Jesus, His Son, to die as a sacrifice for payment of our sins, and how Jesus' blood covers all sins as long as we repent. Bro. Bondage told me he didn't know how I could be a Christian and cut hair at the same time. His wife's hair "had never been touched by scissors." He continuously blubbered from the pulpit that women in pants, short hair, nail polish, jewelry, perfume, or lipstick would never enter heaven. One evening after getting off work, I rushed to church still wearing the pants I had worked in that day. He coldly approached me as I quickly apologized for my apparel. He tersely replied, "Just don't let it happen again." Once a new convert was removed from teaching Sunday school when he found out she served beer at her much-needed waitressing job. She got discouraged and quit coming to church altogether. He also strongly believed there was no room at the foot of the cross for the divorced. I wonder if he thought the blood of Jesus wasn't powerful enough, or God's mercy wasn't rich enough to blot out wrong marriages ... horrible sins, yes ... but not divorces.

Conviction eventually caught up with me, and I had to come clean about my adulterous affair with Jack. I went to Bro. Bondage for help. He was appalled at how far I had "backslidden." I too was very ashamed. He told me to go back to where I left Jesus ... back to when I started wearing pants and makeup again. Now I may be a stupid, country bumpkin, but even I knew that had to be ridiculous!

*   *   *   *   *

Harvey came in late one night while I was sitting in darkness. The girls were tucked in bed and resting peacefully. He sat on the couch with me like he wanted to say something. I decided to beat him to it. "We need to divorce," I said calmly. He nodded his head, not with unsure, sad, slow nods, but with definite, sharp nods. He wouldn't look at me. I told him I would file for divorce that week, and he would have to pay child support. He told me to come to his workplace every Friday evening to collect the money. We agreed I would keep the trailer and the little truck, and he would keep his motorcycle and name brand toolbox full of high-priced tools. There were no other material items to divide. He then looked at me with sad, empty eyes and said, "I'm sorry, Connie Lou, tell the kids I love them." Satan had his claws dug deep into his spirit, and he saw no way of freeing himself from the enemy's grasp, even though he desperately wanted to be loose. Harvey was good material, fine clay when first placed on the Potter's wheel, but the spinning was torment for him. He failed to see the options, the vessel he could become. Instead he chose death, for life without Christ *is* death. He lost sight of love or building love, if not in the marriage and me, at least in the children and the family unit. There had been wonderful moments of love and laughter between us all. We had been through a lot of hardships and remained committed to the idea of marriage, but now it was over. Now, sadly, we chose to give up and move on.

I sat silently on the couch while he packed his toothbrush and a change of clothes. He was reenergized as he prepared to leave for the last time, knowing he didn't have to return to someone he disliked so very much. He spun out on his chopper less than an hour after rumbling in.

God was merciful to bless my daughters and me with a special friendship. We trusted and adored each other. More importantly . . . we *needed* each other.

Chapter Sixteen

I decided to start fresh at a new church closer to my home. Bro. Bondage seemed glad I decided to attend church elsewhere. I felt I didn't meet his standard for congregants. I was a 25-year-old divorcee with a checkered past and shaky future. Despite having much of my family seated in the pews surrounding me and having been raised in that church (as well as several generations before me), Bro. Bondage brushed me off and shamed me on the night that was to be my last attendance there. He told the congregation I had done some terrible things, more than they knew, and would need my prayers. This was all said with a tone of voice that spoke louder than his words . . . to him I was too wayward to ever be a victorious Christian. He tried to pass over the evening without acknowledging me or sending me off with love, but the church members had another plan. After being dismissed, my family and friends waited in line to bid me farewell. We hugged, cried, and prayed together while the sweaty, fat preacher watched in disgust.

The girls and I became members and were quickly involved at the Nazarene Church in Morehead. I volunteered to start a Junior Church program, somewhat like a nursery for the worship hour but with Bible teaching and all ages, except the babies, combined. I had my own children and sometimes over twenty others captivated before me, as I put up flannel graph pictures and shared wonderful Bible stories. They were precious little creatures, and for one hour a week I seriously took their relationship with Jesus as my responsibility . . . one I would account for someday before God. The children grew to trust me, and we shared a certain love that I valued deeply.

I don't remember the lesson I taught that pivotal morning. It was a bright Sunday, 29 May 1989, warm but not hot. The basement where we held Junior Church was comfortably cozy and safe as the kids gathered around me like cattle mingling together under a big shade tree on a hot day. I was nervous about giving an "altar call," an invitation to receive Jesus as Savior. Somehow I stumbled around and asked if anybody wanted to turn their life over to Christ. I was astonished as several hands shot high into the air, their little hands waving to be sure of recognition. Among the converts I led to Jesus that morning were my own two little babies. Jessica was seven, Lacy was five, and they both glowed with new hope. Jessica had been hearing about Jesus since my conversion five years prior. She had witnessed first hand the change it made in me. Lacy was in my womb as the Holy Spirit took up residence in my heart . . . I suppose you could say she witnessed the change as well, perhaps more internally than most. They *were* young and likely don't remember the experience, but it doesn't matter. Their hearts were changed and their thinking changed. It was a beginning to a new way of existing, and I was thrilled!

Going to church and worshipping God became our stabilizer. The pastor was a fun-loving person with a nice wife and two teenage children. He had a jolly laugh and was light-hearted as he presented the gospel. He accepted me where I was in my walk with Christ and invested energy in my children and me. Most of the people there liked me, except for the choir director. Her name was Sondra, and she was married to a board member, which meant she thought she ran the church. I had agreed to head VBS, and we were nearing the close of the session. After having refreshments outside in the parking lot, I called for the kids, perhaps fifty or more, to come inside. Sondra's son was on the far end of the lot, and when he didn't respond to my call I suspected he hadn't even heard me. I yelled his name and told him to come in, using the same manner directed toward all the other children. Once settled inside, the children sat dutifully on the front pews. I stood alone in front of them and was about to close the evening with a song and prayer. I looked up and saw Sondra charging down the aisle like a steaming mad bull! She was glaring at me in contempt with flared nostrils and a clenched jaw. Grabbing her preteen son, she hissed an order for me to never speak to her son like that again. She marched out the door, pulling her rattled youngster along. I was stunned as I tried to maintain composure in front of my young audience and other adult workers. The pastor tried to stop me from calling her with an apology, he was tired of her manipulative, upsetting disposition and wanted to let "her stew." But I insisted on calling her as he stood by and listened. She coldly received my apology, with the condition that I also apologize to her son. She put him on the phone, I explained why I yelled, and I apologized even though it felt very unnecessary and wrong. I hung up and cried in the pastor's office, while my girls waited quietly in the nursery.

I was still working at Marty's Beauty Shop and doing Reflexology (in my office only). Business was booming, but largely because we charged low fees for our services. By the time I was paid my half of the earnings, paid the bills, and bought groceries, the money was gone. Harvey quit paying child support just a few months after the divorce, so except for occasional mechanical assistance, he was little help. Mom and Dad still lived in Olive Hill, ten miles away. They helped with the girls sometimes, but I tried not to bother them too much. Mom was dating her future third husband, Dad and Wanda were still married, and Anna was around 12-years-old. Billy was married and had a little girl. Cindy was divorced from her second husband and had two daughters the same ages as Lacy and Jessica.

A girlfriend set me up to meet a divorced man from our church. His name was Damion B., and he was a singer and talented musician. Damion, along with his brother, sister, and nephew, promoted their own, fairly popular, hometown gospel band. The Nazarene church was his home church, but he was rarely there since he traveled a lot making appearances at festivals, churches, and on Christian television broadcasts. He was short, chubby, and balding, but had a nice smile and seemed to desire a sincere walk with the Lord. I was quite taken by his public guise, but it took me nearly a year to fully realize how loathsome was his private personality.

We were physically involved from the first date. Every Sunday I went to the altar with a broken heart and begged for strength to quit "fooling around." I would emerge with smeared makeup and a swollen face but determined to stay strong . . . which lasted until Friday night's date when both our desires started screaming for attention. My capricious lifestyle *and Satan's craftiness* wielded me as a spiritual yo-yo. I tried incredibly hard to live the Christian life. I deserved an "A for effort," but I lacked something . . . Some crucial part to over-coming sin was not in place. I had no idea what it was. Perhaps it was willpower or self-esteem. Maybe my past branded me inadequate without sex. Possibly it was all natural, acceptable, understandable to be lonely, weak, tired, and a failure in keep-ing God's laws . . . after all, look at what I had been through! Couldn't an attractive, young mother, alone in her own home late at night, make an exception to the rules of holiness? Since God is so good, kind, compassionate, and loving wouldn't He toss me a wink and say, "Go ahead, I was young once too"? As the Apostle Paul would say, "God forbid!" God was indeed merciful to me. I repeatedly disappointed the only person from whom I ever truly felt loved. Instead of final, harsh judgement, in cadence with my defeated actions and burning confessions, Jesus, my best friend, handed out sweet, fragrant forgiveness. He was calling my name, making sure my hand never slipped from His. Mercifully, unrevealed to me, He was gently and strategically shaping me for a future position in His unit of warriors against the darkness through which I then treaded.

Damion was ashamed to be seen in public with a divorced woman and two little children. It wasn't good for his image, so we rarely went out. When we did go out, he was stiff and mean. One time he got mad at one of the girls for embarrass-ing him in a restaurant and he walked out. He left us there to either walk or find a ride home . . . we had to walk. He didn't like us to come to his home either. I'm not sure why. We were there once, and the girls got in to his daughter's room and wanted to play with some of her old toys. His daughter was a teenager and lived with her mother in a distant town. Damion got angry because I insisted he let them play. He grabbed a toy and threw it at the girls. He ordered them out of the room, locked the door, and demanded they stay in the living room with us and sit quietly.

After a few months I only saw Damion late at night, after the kids were put to bed. It was the same routine every time . . . a little shallow talk, become aroused, fight the temptation for a while . . . then we congenially finished the act, and immediately he left.

Once while dating Damion, I got a bad stomach virus that put me in bed, vomiting for three days. Violent dry heaves produced little more than saliva and blood. I wasn't able to work or take care of my children. They ate toaster pastries, peanut butter, and whatever they could find. The dishes were all dirty, the house was a mess, and the girls and I looked equally as bad! Damion finally decided to come check on me, and he even cleaned the kitchen, just enough to soften me towards him. It got late and time for the girls to go to bed. They had been sleeping with me, since I was unable to get up and tuck them in; but that didn't fit into Damion' plan for the evening. He tried to order them off to bed, and they balked. He took off his belt and swung at Lacy (an act of discipline I rarely used myself). Like a fuzzy-tailed bunny, she quickly hopped out of range. He loudly laughed at her bold but frail, little attempt to protect herself. I had tried many nights before to demand he leave, yet knew he *never* left until he got what he wanted. Though extremely ill and bent over from nausea, I got up and put the kids in their beds. When I pushed back the blankets, I exposed myself, braless under a thin, long T-shirt. It was more than enough for Damion to get excited. When I returned to my bed, he swiftly took his pleasures and left. The next morning I called Dad and asked him to take me to the hospital, where I was admitted and treated for nausea and dehydration.

I quit my job at Marty's, moved my Reflexology office and started styling hair in another beauty shop with an ex-Christian lady named Valerie Williams. It was a classy place with higher prices and I hoped to make more money. Damion thought being a hairdresser was a lowly occupation, and he often belittled me. Sometimes with little provoking, he threw fits of rage, spouting out accusations of running a whorehouse, and asking if Valerie and I also provided blow-jobs after the foot massages. A few times he drew back his fist to hit me but stopped short when I ducked and cried out. After each fight and a "three day waiting period," Damion would come see me, carrying an expensive gift and doing his best to be friendly to my children. He was earnest at "petting the calf to catch the cow."

Harvey discovered I had a boyfriend and started threatening both of us. He called several of Damion's family members and told how he was going to murder him if he didn't stay away from me. Damion borrowed a gun from his brother and carried it with him everywhere he went, especially when he visited me. He wrapped it in a towel to conceal it from the neighbors as he walked inside my trailer, then he placed it on top of the refrigerator in my small kitchen adjoining the living room.

Harvey got excessively drunk and decided one night to go see Damion. For some reason, he called me before he left and told me he and one of his friends were going to go kill my boyfriend. I called Damion and warned him. When Harvey got there, he stumbled to the door. Scared spitless, Damion pulled his gun from behind his back and pointed it at Harvey, which made Harvey back off and leave quietly. Harvey and his friend returned to their party house to get a little more soused. I finally reached him on the phone. Harvey was so drunk his speech was slurred and slow, but it was clear he was planning to go back later that night and surprise my "pussy boyfriend." I begged him to come see me before he did anything. That sounds like a stupid move, but I knew Harvey wanted a fight and I could give it to him. Hopefully, it would keep everyone alive. Sure enough, Harvey's bike came roaring up to my front porch, and he staggered up the steps. I opened the door but kept the security chain in place. I tried to talk to him through the four-inch opening. With one swift kick, he broke the chain, and the door flew open as I jumped back. The fight started right away. He had my head locked in his arms as he hurled ugly insults and threats. He told me he was sorry for busting my door and after making several crude remarks, he wrestled me to the couch and began to assault me. When I offered no resistance . . . too broken to care . . . he changed his mind and said, "Ah, I don't want you, you no good . . . !" With disinterest in my life, I spat on his face that loomed a few inches from mine. He was surprised, I was proud of myself, but I prayed God would take care of my children if this terrible fight proved to be my last. He pounded me like wrestlers do on television. He spit in my face several times, each time rubbing it in, blending it with my tears and watery nose, smearing it with intended, painful pressure over my face. I got my hand behind one of his ears and dug in my fingernails. I told him to leave, or I would tear off his ear . . . and I would have! After roughing me up a little longer, and calling me a few more choice names, he finally did leave.

*   *   *   *   *

A woman in our town barely survived an attack from a maniac with a tobacco hatchet. The newspaper reported that the offender was possibly a local person and warned people to exercise caution. Damion lived close to where the attack took place, and for several insignificant reasons, I became fearful he was the criminal.

I was in church a few nights after that brutal incident. Damion was there as well. After church he invited me out to dinner. The girls were visiting one of their grandparents, and so I agreed to meet him at a mutual friend's house. I was sure my imagination was running wild thinking he was the culprit, and it *was* a special treat having an invitation to dinner in a nice restaurant, so I accepted the offer. The evening quickly soured. He wanted to go to his house before we went to eat and wouldn't say why. When we got there I said I would wait in his vehicle while he went in. That made him blow up! His brother lived just a few yards from him and could easily hear and see everything that went on there. That relieved me, but intensified Damion' anxiety. He opened the passenger's door and tried to force me out by pulling my arm. He called me all

kinds of vile names. When that didn't work, he got back inside
the truck and started "sweet talking" me and trying to kiss me.
I jerked away and didn't return his kiss. Again his fury esca-
lated. He jumped out, opened the garage door, and attempted
to drive his truck inside. I considered jumping out and running,
just when he decided the truck wouldn't fit in the garage among
all the sound equipment and junk. His nose started bleeding,
and after blaming me for it, he ran inside to get a towel. He
was very particular about his expensive clothes and didn't want
to ruin the suit he was wearing. After much pleading and my
refusal to fulfill his intentions, he finally returned me to my
truck that was parked at our friends' house and then followed
me as I pulled out. I was afraid to go home, so I made a
desperate decision to drive by Harvey's rented house and stop
if I had to. It was a crazy plan, but I knew Damion was afraid
of Harvey and his wild buddies, and I was sure I could get rid
of him there. When I turned down Harvey's street, Damion
went on.

I hardly saw Damion after that, and I never went out on a
date with him again. I'll never know for sure why he insisted I
go inside his house that night, but I suspect, in reality, he
simply hoped for an *appetizer* before dinner. He found another
girlfriend and our courtship was over, but our connection was
yet to undergo an appalling, final sever.

Chapter Seventeen

I picked up a second job as a bookkeeper at a department store near the university campus. I still worked in the salon, but I was starting to have problems related to the various hair solutions used on customers. The skin on my hands peeled continuously and left red, sore spots. My nose had sores inside from inhaling chemicals. Every night my arms, back, legs, and feet ached from the day's work, and I was tired of listening to customers gossip and whine. So a quiet desk job was a blessing. I worked in a small office with two ladies that attended a booming charismatic church in town called Word of Life. Tracy was the pastor's wife, Robin was active in the children's programs, and I was a misfit still hanging on at the Nazarene Church. They invited me to church with them, so I decided to go to their New Year's Eve service. I sat motionless while people hopped and jitterbugged, screaming wildly while running, jumping, and lifting arms high, as if reaching for or receiving something. Some people appeared to pass out and lie on the floor, seemingly in a trance, while others walked over and around them. I heard a lot of "tongues" that night, utterances that were distinctly different from each other but supposedly spoken directly to God while somewhat bypassing the human intellect. It was a little more than I was prepared to accept. As I left, they handed me pamphlets that presented scriptural examples and spiritual reasons for everything I had seen. I thought it was more emotionalism than spiritualism, but decided to visit the church again . . . at least they *were* awake!

I still slept with a Bible under my pillow and had a crippling terror of night noise. I had seen a lot of trash in churches. Actually I had seen as much junk happen in, and related to, church as I did out in the world. I told God I was sick of it. If that was all He had to offer, I wasn't interested. If this all-powerful God couldn't produce a "body of Christ" any better than this, then He must not be "All that!" I was kneeling in my bedroom beside the bent, rusted air vent that blew out winter's heat. The spirit of God seemed glad I had opened my heart to him like I would to a trusted friend. He seemed to appreciate my honesty, and He placed a statement in my heart . . . "I will show you who I AM."

That night I decided to remove the Bible from under my pillow. It was a test, which I was sure God would fail. I turned out the lights, crawled in bed, and snuggled my head into the pillow. For seven years, I trusted the lump under my head to protect me from the evil that emerged in the dark of night. I waited for sleep to slip in. It usually took over an hour. I dreaded the ugly goons that would appear the moment I slipped off. I was impressed when the fresh morning light awakened me after a restful night's sleep. I realized I hadn't awakened each time the furnace kicked on or a car drove by. "Okay, God, that was pretty cool," I thought, but I was not overly excited.

Robin and Tracy didn't seem particularly interested in beating me with the Bible. They just went about their work as though Jesus was literally in the room. We had a new computer system that gave all of us a hard time. One day Tracy's computer screen blitzed into all kinds of scribbles scrolling at terrific speed. Our office manager was a temperamental, stressed-out jerk. None of us wanted to approach him with computer problems or *any* problem, so it was important that we did our jobs well and not involve him. Tracy shrieked and threw her hands back as I turned to see what happened. She immediately grabbed the monitor, like one might grab a child about to tumble over a high ledge, and began to pray. She *commanded* it to work properly in *Jesus' name*. I was about to laugh when the screen came to a halt and the appropriate data reestablished itself on the monitor. She sighed and thanked God, as I raised my eyebrows and went back to work.

Robin was a real trooper. The way she marched to everything she did amused me. She was a woman *with a past*, married to an unsettled husband, and had two sons that found trouble too easily. She lived in a run-down shack, drove a run-down jalopy . . . and loved Jesus and served Him with all her heart. In the office, she handled accounts payable, which was an especially demanding position. Once the manager came in and told her to run a particular report for a certain span of time in the year, something like "from September 7, 8:00 A.M. to the end of the year." He was adamant about wanting it by the end of the day. Asking the computer to give that information shouldn't have been difficult, but for some reason, it would only give her data for the entire year. The printer wouldn't run unless its lid was down, even though the computer continued to process information and move through its task. Annoyed and needing to get her work done, Robin decided to allow the computer to run the report for the entire year. The printer was loud, and to print out that much data for a whole year would have reaped a printout over six inches high and taken most of the day. She decided she would leave up the printer lid up and keep an eye on the screen. When it approached the needed date she would put the lid down and begin printing the report. The morning passed and we went to lunch. The computer was slow and still months away from September when we returned. By late afternoon we were all diligently involved in our work. Robin was working at another station, since her computer was tied up. She suddenly jumped up and shouted, "Oh, no!" as she ran to the printer and slammed down the lid. She didn't bother to look at the screen to see where it was at in retrieval of information. She knew it had to be close or well past the needed date. Tracy and I glanced at each other with worry, knowing what was happening and hoping she hadn't missed the needed beginning date. We ran to the printer and watched with Robin while it inked out the first line . . . beginning precisely with the first transaction dated 7 September 1988, 8:00 A.M.!

*   *   *   *   *

Jessica was in the second grade and Lacy in kindergarten. They rarely got to see Harvey. I tried to arrange visits with him, but they usually fell through. Several times he would commit to visiting them, only to be gone when I took them there. The girls would climb out of their seat belts and jump up and down in their seats as we approached his house. They knew Harvey was great at playing and entertaining them, a skill I had to polish after we split up. I was the one who worked and was gone while he stayed home and got to watch them play and grow, at least for the first few years. As we would approach his house, we could tell if he was home or had skipped out. Many times as I pulled in front of his empty house, I watched their little hearts sink. Disheartened, they slid down into the seat and waited while I knocked on the door, receiving no response. I tried to cheer them up by taking them on adventures in the woods or by the lake. I always told them their father loved them. He just had so many problems that he couldn't see his way out. It made me angry that he didn't make time for them, and I tried to force him to see them. I got tired of seeing the girls hurt and quit trying to make it happen. They were incredibly strong during that time. In the past, when they asked where Daddy was, I lied and told them he was working. During most of our fierce arguments they were safely in bed, protected from it all. So it was hard for them to understand why he wasn't around any more. I simply didn't have the words or knowledge to explain the situation in a way that would ensure their emotional stability and health. God became their counselor *and* father . . . *and He did an excellent job.* After that realization, I determined to never again lie to my children. Regardless of how difficult, I began being painfully honest with them and respecting their ability to grasp weighty issues. I have no regrets. Today we have an open trust that all of us enjoy with each other.

One evening Robin stopped by my trailer to visit. Our kids played around our feet while we talked and laughed like giddy schoolgirls. It was nearing bedtime as I stood at my front door bidding Robin and her boys a good night. Just as I shut the door, Jessica said, "Mommy, what is that?" I turned toward the back of the trailer, toward the two little girls' bedrooms, and the top eighteen inches of air space next to the ceiling was full of smoke! I ran to the back to locate the source. It was coming from the wall in Jessica's closet. I called 911 and waited for the fire department. I had heard that old mobile homes could be engulfed in flames in less than three minutes. I sat the girls together in a living room chair close to the front exit, as I went to get the photo albums for safekeeping. I considered gathering up clothes and other necessities to pack in the car . . . instead I sat in the living room with the girls on my lap and prayed. We were singing "Jesus loves me" when the fire engines screamed into our neighborhood. They were dressed in the same attire used to fight the fire at the egg factory. Their oversized boots and black rubber coats made their manly frames larger than life and made my twelve-foot by sixty-foot mobile home seem like a playhouse. They tromped over toys and worn carpet with little regard as they searched for a way to stop the smoldering before it ignited into an inferno. It was raining outside, so the girls and I stayed out of the way on the couch, continuing to sing softly. I desperately needed God to save my home.

Ora and Opal were my elderly neighbors who loaned me tools and sugar. They loved us dearly, as we did them. I heard Ora call out, "Connie! What's wrong?" I stepped out onto the porch to explain the situation. Ora and Opal were dripping wet, and some other neighbors had assembled with umbrellas. I tried to assure Ora it would be all right and to go back inside. Of course, he wouldn't and begged us to go to his house. The smoke dissipated, and the firemen essentially gave up. They said to call them back when, or if flames broke out. Despite Ora's pleas, I decided to stay in the trailer that night. I hoped that if I kept a close watch, I could extinguish any flames before they destroyed our home. My bedroom was on the opposite end of the trailer from the children's rooms and farthest from the source of smoke. There I bedded down the girls, directly under a window through which we could easily escape if necessary. I stayed awake the entire night, watching carefully for accumulated smoke. Every few minutes, I examined each room, checking the walls for heat by using my palms as detectors. The smoke never reappeared. I spent many nights after that, lying awake and checking for signs of fire. The girls slept in my bed for several weeks, until I was sure all danger was passed. Eventually we trusted God for our safety, thanked Him, and gave Him the credit for watching over us and preserving our home.

*   *   *   *   *

There was a young girl that started working part time in the office. She invited Robin and me to come to a birthday party arranged for her brother, whom she wanted me to meet. Harvey was then living in a small camper that sat in a parking lot behind the garage where he worked. I decided to ask him to baby-sit. It was an absurd idea, but I hoped enough time had passed, and it might actually work. He was there when we arrived, and the girls ran off to play with some children they knew from school. We talked civilly while he showed me the camper his Dad had given him. He was completely sober and even had food in the small refrigerator.

I arrived at the birthday party at the same time Robin did. Neither of us really wanted to be there, but we smiled and made our appearance. When the beer came out, we offered our excuses and left. It was still daylight, a pleasant summer evening, as Robin and I walked to our cars. Her husband was playing softball with the church team at the park, and she invited me to go with her to watch them play. I wasn't interested, especially when she grinned and said there was a really cute guy that played every week, and she thought he was single. "Great!" I thought with irritation, "Matched up twice in one night." I told her I needed to put gas in the car, and then I might come out for a while. Since I had a baby-sitter and I didn't know what else to do, I decided to drive to the park. When I got there nobody was around. I almost gave up and started to go pick up the girls, when I remembered there was another ballpark outside of town. For the fun of it, I decided to drive out and see if I could find it.

It was a nice area, near a tobacco warehouse, with a ball diamond and bleachers. There were a lot of cars in the lot, and

I was afraid I couldn't find Robin. I was uncomfortable as I walked up to an unknown crowd of people, but as I got closer I began to recognize some of them from Robin and Tracy's church. Several of them greeted me as I found Robin and planted myself next to her. We were standing at the end of the bleachers near the players. Robin's husband, Kevin, walked over to us with a big smile. I sensed something was up. "Do you want to meet that guy over there?" he abruptly asked as he pointed toward the bench full of players on the other side of the foul line fence. "Not really," I said. "Thanks anyhow." It's amazing how single people are treated. It seems the instant you're officially single, or people discover you're unattached, the hunt or chase begins. Kevin and Robin smiled mischievously and convinced me to walk over to the fence and at least say, "Hello." The three of us strolled over and stood behind the players wearing Word of Life T-shirts. They were laughing and having a great time with each other. Kevin yelled at one of the players as he turned to face us.

My heart stopped as I smiled and flushed. His name was Kelly and he was quite handsome! He was just a little taller than I, tanned, muscular, dark-haired, and looking right at me with a huge grin on his incredible face! We awkwardly said, "Hello," as all the guys starting making wise cracks and whistling. It was obvious the attraction was immediate and electrifying, but I was nervous and tired of men. Robin and I went back to the bleachers and watched the remainder of the game. Kevin was the mediator. He went back and forth delivering messages like on an elementary playground. After the game, Robin, Kevin, Kelly, and I decided to stop at a fast-food restaurant for a late snack. As we walked toward our cars together, I mentioned I couldn't stay long because I had to get home to my kids. I saw Kelly's face drop. I assumed he wasn't told that I had two little toddlers, so I felt certain that was the end of that. We got to the restaurant, and I ordered coffee to help me finish the night's duties waiting for me at home. The others ordered ice cream. Kelly and I began gathering background information. He was the foreman and master plumber for a large, reputable construction company in town. The owners of the company were distant family members and had convinced him to come there to work after a hailstorm in western Kansas left his crops destroyed and him in great debt.

He was 32-years-old, had never been married, and had no children. He had been in Kentucky for six years and deeply longed to be back on the plains of Kansas. He was a nice guy that had hardly seen or felt heartache. He deserved someone with less baggage than what I carried, and I was sure, given enough time, he would eventually determine that himself. I knew my story was too sordid for the moment, so I started with the basics . . . I was divorced, had two little girls, and worked two jobs as a hairdresser and bookkeeper. He was relieved to know I was divorced. He was afraid Kevin had fixed him up with a married woman, which was the reason for the long expression back in the parking lot. We laughed at that. Kelly asked if I had pictures of my girls. Of course I did and was glad to show them off. He took his time as he looked at them carefully and thoughtfully. My heart melted when he tenderly touched the glossy photos and smiled softly. As we stood to leave the restaurant, Kelly touched the tip of my nose with his ice cream cone, leaving a dot of white, sticky stuff for me to wipe off. We laughed as he licked his cone and said, "Call me sometime." "You call *me*," I said, thinking that would be more appropriate. He said he would, and with that we parted.

Chapter Eighteen

After the four of us left the restaurant, I drove straight to Harvey's camper. Several cars were parked around it. Music and crude voices blared from within. I knocked on the door and someone tipsy opened it. Thick smoke rolled out the opening into the night air. There sat my babies among that crowd of degenerates and heavy sin. "What was I thinking!" I shouted inside my head. "How could I have left them with him? I should have known what would happen! What if one of those creeps tried to hurt them?" I took their little hands and led them out of the thick air. I simply told Harvey, "Good bye," and left. I knew I would never again ask him to baby-sit or visit the children.

Back at home they were bathed and put to bed just before the phone rang. It was Kelly. We talked and laughed for hours. He had a super sense of humor and loved to make me laugh.

Later that week Kelly sent me a dozen red roses at work. That was too fast for me, and I was aloof when he popped in the door to see how I liked them. I wasn't about to be wined and dined, then hop in the sack again. He was confused, but didn't give up.

We went out several times before I allowed him to meet Jessica and Lacy. Then I decided it was time to let them check him out. Kids have a special gift of perception, and I appreciated their intuition. When he pulled up, we were outside on the porch. He popped out of his sunroof, smiling and acting silly. The kids loved it! I felt restless and apprehensive as I watched them fall in love with him.

Kelly, the girls, and I were together several times a week. We both wanted to keep the relationship light and pure before God. We went to church together and took the children to fantastic places like the circus, Christian concerts, and to the lake for fishing and hiking. We had been dating for three months before we nervously permitted a quick kiss.

Chapter Nineteen

Harvey learned I was dating Kelly and knew who he was through one of his drinking friends. He hassled us a little, but nothing too violent. The worst he did to Kelly was scratch obscenities on the door of his beautiful, super sport Monte Carlo.

As if I didn't have enough problems, Damion decided he was jealous and wanted me back. He drove past my trailer numerous times to make sure I didn't have company. He called and tried to get me to come to his house for a swim in his pool. I wanted nothing to do with him, and that outraged him. Kelly and I were sitting on my living room couch one evening when Damion abruptly threw open my front door and stepped in! I asked Kelly to leave so Damion and I could talk. I knew it disappointed Kelly to see me choose to be with Damion instead of him, but my first concern was for his physical well being. I wanted to handle Damion alone, and didn't want to see Kelly get hurt. Kelly was far more muscular than Damion, as well as more agile and clever. He could have easily taken on a fight and won, but I didn't want to put him in that situation. Besides, I wasn't sure Damion would fight fair . . . I knew his gun had to be close by. So Kelly hung his head and left. I was too occupied to wonder for long if he would ever come back.

Damion and I talked without shouting. The girls were in bed, and he didn't want to wake them and have to wait while I resettled them. He started making moves on me, which I rejected. I was cold and unaroused. He became more agitated and tried every threat he could think of to make me have sex with him. Then he threatened to hurt Jessica or Lacy or have them taken away from me. After being raped once, I had always declared it would never happen again. Somehow I would gouge out the perpetrator's eyes or remove a testicle, but I would *not* be raped again. Incredibly, I remained silent as he forced me into my bedroom. Withdrawn from reality . . . frozen without emotion . . . he raped and pilfered my weary heart and desolate body.

I told Kelly about it right away, as though admitting to cheating on our relationship. I had tried all I knew to prevent it from happening, but to no avail. Kelly wasn't angry, he was strangely consoling. We were both unsure of what to do next or how to feel. Several nights later Damion showed up again. I guess he thought he would get away with the same routine, but I wasn't up for it. He burst through the door and started yelling obscenities. I stood up and confronted him, leaving Kelly seated on the couch a few feet in front of us. Damion grabbed my face and locked his pursed lips against mine. I struggled free and called him names. He rammed his hand between my legs and tried to pull me to the bedroom. I wondered who was going to flip out first and prayed Kelly would remain still and let me take the brunt of the fight. I felt disgust when I realized he actually wanted Kelly to watch him rape me. I got loose and ran out the door, feeling it was safer outdoors in my busy neighborhood, and hopefully the neighbors would call the police. I got to my car and said I was leaving. I knew he would follow me, and maybe this scene would play out somewhere away from Kelly's eyesight. Damion grabbed me and slapped me with his full strength. Before my head turned back to face him, he backhanded me on the other cheek, which caused me to lose my footing and strike my head against my opened car door. The impact of my skull against metal made a loud crack. My head rang, and I battled to stay alert and not pass out. I wasn't sure what I heard because my head was shrilling a high-pitched tone loudly in my ears. Through the ringing in my head I could hear Kelly. He raised his voice and stated with simple authority, "That's enough!" Jessica was standing in the doorway and crying for her Mommy. I looked toward her, just as Kelly picked her up and held her in his arms. I knew he would watch out for her if this turned out horribly bad. Damion turned on his heels, got in his hot, red Corvette, and drove away. I ran to Jessica and took her back to bed. I lay with her for a long time, listening and waiting. Kelly stayed on the couch until I got up and rejoined him. I told him it was safe to leave, that I'd be all right, Jessica was fine, and as far as I could tell, Lacy had fortunately slept through it all. We didn't try to talk, it was late, and I was tired.

The next day I went to the courthouse and filed assault charges against Damion. The police apprehended him at his workplace, but soon released him after assigning a date to appear in court and answer to the charges. Damion wasted no time rallying support from the Nazarene Church. He called Sondra right away and convinced her to hound me to drop the charges. He called the pastor and asked him to visit him. The pastor went to his home and evidently spent several hours listening to Damion lay out dirty details of our relationship, while adding embellishments along the way. The pastor never asked to speak to me or offered to hear my side of the story. Instead, he stood in the pulpit the following Sunday and venomously denounced me. That was after he publicly ordered the Junior Church students and I to remain on the front pews throughout his "sermon," instead of going downstairs as usual. Those little children and *my* children listened while he raked me over the coals. According to him, I deserved to be punished. It was wrong to be in sin and hold an important title as Sunday school teacher . . . certainly a valid response, but the children didn't deserve the disappointment and confusion of the moment. For their own sakes, I pray none of them remember that dark day.

After a lot of pressure from the church, I dropped the charges against Damion, just moments before he stood in front of the judge. Someone in the courtroom told me later that Damion laughed when the judge called him forward and announced the charges had been dismissed.

I went to the Nazarene Church one last time and told the little ones and my close friends, "Good bye." I later heard that the pastor quit the ministry and was no longer serving the Lord . . . I hope it's not true.

*   *   *   *   *

I was at Vicky's, trying to work through some late, night appointments, when one of my customers, an elderly lady, said to me something profound and life-changing. She was rambling on and on about herself when I tuned in just as she mumbled, ". . . but the only regret I have is that I lived in the shadows of a university all my life and never got an education." In my heart, I slammed down my scissors and comb and marched straight to the university admissions office. It was settled instantaneously. That fall I was going back to school!

I started making inquiries about what to do to get enrolled. I was told that I could qualify for welfare, food stamps, and government grants and loans except for one problem. I still owned three acres of land that was considered an asset, too much to qualify for assistance. However if I lived *on* the land it would be considered my home and not necessarily an asset. I made a quick, drastic decision to move my trailer back upon the hill from where I had drug it a few years earlier.

I set up the movers and everything needed to get us there. I unblocked the trailer and tore off the underpinning myself. Dad helped remove and transport the porch. Kelly had gone to Kansas to visit his family and hardly knew anything about my decision. When he returned, the trailer was gone, and a lot of stuff needing to be moved by truck was left lying around the rented lot. I borrowed Dad's ugly, old, rusted-out, orange, pickup truck and started in. Kelly pulled up just as I was about to leave with a full load. I had on worn-out tennis shoes with holes in them. My hair and face were undone, and my clothes were ragged and stained. I was concerned it might turn him off, but I decided it was time he saw what real life with me would be like. I was a hard worker, not a prissy, don't-break-a-nail, perfect lady. I had been raised rough and had led a rough life, unlike his *so-called*, "All-American," perfect family history. I didn't enjoy cooking and wasn't looking for somebody else to take care of. I knew I had to stay focused on the ultimate goal and not get distracted or pulled down by dead weight. At the time, that goal was to get through school with a degree and take care of my girls with as little opposition as possible. Kelly could either fit in or get lost . . . it really didn't matter to me. Kelly hopped in the truck and rode with me to my new address. I expected him to disappear after seeing the squalor to which I had moved my children. The trailer was sitting sideways after Dad had tried to level it with some old jacks and one of them broke, nearly crushing him underneath. He simply dropped the task and told me to get somebody else to do it. Kelly was eager to help unload the truck and even crawled under the trailer and began the tedious chore of leveling my humble home. I was grateful, but remained cautious.

The electric company had agreed to set poles and run electricity to our mobile home, but that would take three weeks to accomplish. I had no running water and had no plans of being able to get it any time soon. My sewer pipe was run from the toilet to a hole I had dug with Dad's shovel and covered with a board. I used my little hatchback car to fetch buckets of water from the pond for flushing the toilet. A service station in town generously allowed me to stop everyday and fill empty milk containers from their outdoor faucet for bathing and consumption.

My stove and furnace were run by gas, so I needed to get a propane tank set up. That required a ninety dollar deposit, which I didn't readily have. It was late summer and heat wasn't needed yet. That would just leave the problem of a stove. Aunt Helen and Uncle Junior insisted that I needed a cook stove. These two were special to me for several reasons, mostly spiritual.

Uncle Junior was an ex-cop that patrolled the local State Park where my friends and I used to cruise and hide while we fried our brains with alcohol and drugs. Eight years earlier he had found my brother's van loaded down with stoned teenagers (including me), parked next to a public area in the park where he was employed. When he had pulled up and banged on the side door to get our attention over the deafening music, we hardly cared if it was the police or Godzilla. Somebody slid back the door, and there stood my uncle. He could have easily arrested us all (and it appeared as though he might), until his eyes caught sight of Billy and me. He spoke to us, and we mumbled something back, trying to pretend sobriety. He looked hurt as his thoughts, responsibilities, and Godly love clashed. He told the driver to move on, as he turned away and slid the door closed. Our friends made jokes and extolled us for "having connections." I was ashamed.

Helen and Junior are two of the Garvin Ridge saints, always there for every service and handing out lots of smiles and hugs. They were in church the morning I turned over my heart to Christ, and they continued to be interested in my growth as a Christian. Aunt Helen had a dream the night before my salvation experience in which a young, pretty, girl came to know the Lord personally. The name of the girl in her dream was Katie Albright, a connection I have yet to make. Without pomp, they gave the girls and I a one hundred dollar check. Ninety dollars to use for the propane deposit, and ten dollars to tithe to the Lord. That was one blessing I will never forget.

Chapter Twenty

A special speaker came for a week-long session at Word of Life Church, where I frequently attended with my new friends. He was an exciting presenter of the spiritual gifts God lays before His people. Kelly was "spirit-filled" and had been trying to make me more receptive to speaking in tongues and operating in other spiritual gifts, such as love, faith, wisdom, knowledge, healing, miracles, prophecy, discernment of spirits, various kinds of tongues, and interpretation of tongues. These were Biblical teachings that had never been opened up before me. I found them intriguing but remained skeptical. Kelly, the girls, and I went the first night. I listened and watched the speaker intently as he told a lot of fantastic, unbelievable stories about miracles he had witnessed. It was late when Kelly drove us ten miles out of town and deep into the woods to our trailer on the hill.

At that time, the girls had a white kitten with blue eyes that had been dropped off at our house. His name was Snowboy. He was a pet that was part of our hearts. We pulled up in front of the trailer and heard Snowboy yelping loudly in the dark. He hesitantly appeared and crept inside as he continued to howl deeply and painfully. There was a four-inch stick, the size of my little finger, protruding from one of his eyes. Kelly got a pair of work gloves from his company truck and seized Snowboy in a tight grip. The girls and I prayed. With one quick jerk, Kelly removed the twig and let the cat loose. Snowboy darted behind the couch and quietly crouched there for solace. I was sure he would make a bloody mess, but I humanely let him rest there. The four of us held hands and prayed Snowboy would not die, and his eye wouldn't be blinded. The next morning, Snowboy was meowing and asking for attention as usual. There wasn't a drop of blood anywhere to be found . . . and Snowboy's blue eyes were perfectly normal! We knew that our prayer had been answered.

The second night at church that week, the evangelist spoke about the fire of God. It was particularly interesting to me because of the way fire had destroyed, *or attempted to destroy,* so much in my life. At 2:00 A.M. that night my smoke alarm went off in my trailer. There was no smoke and I found no hot spots in the walls. For emergency calls to the country, the fire department charged a fee, which I couldn't afford, so I was reluctant to notify them. Shaken up, I called Kelly and asked for advice. He told me to remove the batteries from the screaming smoke alarm, and he would be right over. It was nearly dawn by the time we had checked everything, and we felt assured of no danger. Kelly left, having to drive straight to work. It felt good to have a man I could rely on.

The third night at church things really started happening. Small children received the gift of tongues as crystal-clear tears streamed down their soft, innocent faces. People were slain in the Spirit by groups, with their eyes closed and with no prompting or possible clue as to faking it. A demonic spirit was cast out of a woman as she gurgled loud, hideous groans.

That night as sleep eluded me, my mind tumbled over and over as I attempted to decipher all that I had seen and heard. My smoke alarm went off again at 2:00 A.M. I took it down, and after praying, I felt the Spirit of the Lord tell me to not worry about fire. I believe He told me fire would never again harm my family, even though Satan was hot on my trail to destroy me. I purchased a new smoke alarm and new batteries *and* thanked God for not needing them.

I never got the nerve to go forward for prayer that week at church, but it was the beginning of a spiritual awakening. My prayers were changing from beaten-begging to bold-believing. I started going to a women's Bible study where I met Avi Schulman, an elderly, gentle lady that knew I needed more spiritual, overcoming power and strength than what I had. She invited me to her home for one-on-one discipling. She quickly pointed out that the gift of tongues is accessible to everyone. Get your Bible and follow this . . . it's very exciting!

Acts 1:4-5: before Jesus' ascension into Heaven, He tells His apostles to wait in Jerusalem for a gift or promise. That promise was baptism in the Holy Spirit. By verse 8 Jesus tells them they will receive power when the Holy Spirit comes upon them. Acts 2:1-4 describes the scene, as "*all* of them were filled with the Holy Spirit and began to speak in other tongues as the Spirit enabled them." As Peter begins preaching, throughout chapter two, he explains what's happening and what they need to do. In verses 37-38 the people were ready to hear, "Repent! . . . *And* you will receive the gift of the Holy Spirit." The next verse says, "The promise is for *you* and your children and for *all* who are far off . . . for *all* whom the Lord our God will call." I'm certainly not a Bible scholar and wouldn't dare pretend to be one, so check this out for yourself. It won't take a lot of effort to find enough material to help establish your own thinking on this matter. Nonetheless, I'll continue telling my story.

Avi and I held hands and prayed that I would receive the indwelling of the Holy Spirit and walk in fruitful power. When I began to pray in other tongues (my "Heavenly language" as she called it), I became very warm and flushed. I knew the Holy Spirit was doing a work in my spirit. I had to pick up my children from school so Avi walked me to my car, encouraging me to let the Lord have His way. I drove down the street, bursting with excitement. I turned the corner just a few blocks from the school when the joy I felt inside *had* to come out! Like a pot that spills over, I started speaking praises to God in an unintelligible, surrealistic, divine language! That was exciting enough, but instantly all colors around me became crisper and brighter. Even brown light poles took on beautiful hues of dark tones. Grass was greener, pedestrians' clothing became rich with brilliance, and even subtle things gone unnoticed before now blazed with incredible rays of colors. The blueness of the sky is impossible for me to describe. I doubt any author could equitably capture the account. A friend of mine described her experience of receiving the Holy Spirit as being covered with liquid love. Others claimed hearing a ". . . rushing mighty wind, and it filled all the house . . . and . . . cloven tongues like as of fire . . . sat upon each of them." (Acts 2:2-3 KJV). Our eyes were opened . . . Are yours?

Chapter Twenty-One

Ten years after graduating from high school, at age twenty-eight, I returned to college. I quit both jobs and enrolled in an Elementary Education program, taking six credit hours above the considered full-time load of twelve hours. I received several grants and took out student loans to pay tuition and buy books. I received five hundred dollars a month in welfare, two hundred dollars a month in food stamps, and qualified for a medical card that made provisions for any medical necessity the children and I may encounter. My gratitude was immense. I *was* somewhat embarrassed, but continually reminded myself it wasn't a permanent crutch. It was for me, and my kind of situation, for which these government programs were established. To the politicians who strive to keep it workable, I say "Thank you" . . . to the scoundrels who abuse it, may I suggest to you that you are playing with fire and are sure to get burned, one way or another.

It was difficult juggling my school schedules, studying demands, and responsibilities at home, but after the girls and I got used to the pace, things smoothed out. Kelly borrowed a backhoe from his company and, at his own expense, installed a septic system before our first winter on the hill. God was very good to the girls and I, as He dropped miracles along the way.

*   *   *   *   *

I commuted ten miles to school and after dropping off the girls at their grade school, I had to find a parking spot, which was usually a long walk from campus. I carried an armful of books with my Bible *always* on top of the stack. Whenever guys tried to flirt or strike up a conversation with me, I turned it toward Jesus and asked if they knew Him. It was a great way to get out of awkward moments, as well as locate the Christians and hang together. I also discovered a new breed of creep, the kind that gets a thrill from bringing down the good folks. They take it as a challenge, a game that must be won. And once they succeed in making you fail, they strut away with cocky, haughty arrogance.

One of the acquaintances I made at school was a blind boy who walked the same route I did between classes. His name was Tony and, for a few minutes everyday, I pretended to escort him while we chatted about insignificant things. He usually asked about my Jessica and Lacy, and I asked him about his life. I told him I didn't see how he managed all he does and not be able to see. He replied, "You do it or you die." I fully understood.

Philosophy was a required course and one I dreaded. I had heard stories about long, boring lectures on the subject of God's existence and, for that matter, whether or not *we* exist. My first problem was that I hate being bored. Well, actually, I refuse to be bored. And the second problem you can probably figure out on your own. So in order to keep myself entertained in Philosophy class, I posed ponderous theories that exasperated the instructor and annoyed classmates who wanted to take their notes and get out of there without having to think. While debating the evidence presented in proof of God's omnitude, I wondered out loud how he (the instructor) could explain away (which is what he was trying to do) the way God changes people. "For instance," I was half playing as I continued, "I used to be a heavy drinker and abused drugs, but my relationship with Jesus radically changed my desires and even physical addictions. How do you suppose that could happen without a sovereign, all-powerful, and loving entity?" Some girl from the back spoke up in a "valley-girl" accent. Chirping like an irritating bird, she said, "Well, maybe it was a transference of addiction." At first I was upset that she would belittle something so miraculous, likening my relationship with Jesus to my relationship with sin. But then I guess I *was* addicted to Jesus. I needed

Him even worse than I needed drugs. I considered it a good thing to be addicted to serving, loving, worshipping, and examining Jesus. I *had* to have Him, for without Him I preferred death. A few years later, Carmen, a popular Christian musician coined the phrase and wrote a song titled "Addicted to Jesus."

Chapter Twenty-Two

That first winter in the woods was mild. Praise God! Since Dad and Wanda now lived so close to me, we each grew dependent on the other. They were having a lot of problems, and sometimes Dad unloaded on me. He often came to my trailer wanting to borrow money, but of course, I didn't have any. Every penny (literally) of my money was tightly budgeted. I always tithed the top ten percent of my welfare check and grant money (I know that's questionable, but I simply felt I needed to), then every gallon of gasoline and milk was accounted for. Most times I prepared meals in quantities to serve the children only and I would eat if there were leftovers. That was a nutritionally bad plan but worked wonders for my figure.

Anyhow, during one of Dad's visits and after I had no money to loan him, he erupted and spouted about how I was a bad mother. Screaming obscenities and grasping at any insult that might gouge deeply, he spewed, ". . . and YOU can't even provide a decent bath for your CHILDREN!" Ironically, he also was without running water for *his* family.

By spring, Kelly was pushing me to accept his offer to run city water to my trailer. It was a project that would normally cost close to five thousand dollars. Haunted by past poor judgements and perverted people, I played it cool and waited till it felt right. I didn't want to get too indebted to Kelly, in case our relationship fell apart. Burned by a few mistakes of his own, Kelly was also scared of marriage, and the responsibility of children overwhelmed him. Therefore, he didn't seem to be making long-term plans. I needed a husband and a father for my children, not a boyfriend that bought our affection. I grew

more leery of him when I discovered he liked to drink beer
after a hot day on the construction site . . . not a major problem for most American couples, but definitely a halting factor
for me. I'd seen Satan use alcohol as a destructive tool too
many times. I wanted nothing to do with it. Kelly and I talked
and prayed about the problem several times, and we looked to
the Word of God for answers. After a while, the Lord worked
it out, and we both agreed that alcohol would have no part in
our lives together.

I decided to apply for a loan through a low-income housing authority to pay the initial cost of running water nearly a
quarter mile from the county's main supply line. I was ap-
proved fifteen hundred dollars for the city fees and to purchase
pipe. My payments were approximately twenty-seven dollars a
month for five years. I now felt a little more self-reliant and
comfortable with moving forward on Kelly's offer. Dad was
upset. He had hopes of obtaining water from Rowan County,
not Carter County where we lived. Our homes were near the
county line, and Rowan County water was proven to be better
in quality and service. He owned over a hundred acres which
were for sale as building lots, and Rowan County water would
improve their value much more (in his opinion) than would
Carter County water. He believed if I installed water from
Carter County, it would greatly diminish his chances of con-
vincing Rowan County to cross the line and supply him the
valued commodity. It was a hot issue to the folks in that neck
of the woods. He told me I would never get enough water
pressure atop my high hill from Carter County's dilapidated
water system, or they would renege on their promise to maintain the line once it was in place. When that was unsuccessful
in hampering my plans, he told me he wouldn't allow Kelly to
cross his property line with the backhoe and pipe; and if Kelly
ignored Dad's demand, he would get the sheriff *or his shotgun*
and stop him. I had been there nine months without water (not
to mention during the earlier years) and was deaf to his selfish
complaints and threats. Though I was disappointed that he
would behave so heartlessly toward me, as well as his grandchildren, I discounted it all as unfortunate ploys and continued
with the plan.

I went to the city municipal building to pay the fees for the water meter and tap. I had completed the application several months prior but didn't pay the fees until things were in place. My excitement turned bleak when the secretary informed me the fees had raised from one hundred seventy-five dollars to five hundred dollars, effective as of "*yesterday!*" God showed mercy through the secretary as she decided it would be appropriate to complete my file according to the date on the initial application for service.

The day finally came . . . and so did the backhoe and a truckload of two-inch, high-pressure water line, as well as several rolls of black, one-inch water line for my only neighbor in sight. She was an old, wrinkled countrywoman with several unruly, grown boys and had also lived many years without running water in her shack of a home. Kelly thought it only made sense to install a line for her in the same ditch as ours. This gesture of Christianity left her utterly and, I must say, beautifully speechless. I'm sure Kelly would say her expression of gratitude was worth every cent. The deed to my property included a forty-foot right-of-way along the road, so Kelly was careful to stay off Dad's property and within that boundary, even though it meant taking a more dangerous route along the steep hillside. The sheriff never showed up and neither did Dad with his shotgun, as he had threatened.

It was late and raining when we ran to the kitchen faucet to try it out. Kelly and his good friend, Mark, who came to help free of charge, as well as the girls and I, were covered in yellow, Kentucky clay mud. We were all exuberant with joy *and* weariness, but there it was: not black "gold" as unearthed by the Beverly Hillbillies, but clear, clean, liquid "gold" . . . and not a weak trickle as forecasted by Dad, but a strong, abundant flow supplying forceful pressure. Kelly and Mark finished up outside while the girls and I played in the bathtub. Jessica and Lacy were exhausted and easily fell asleep once they settled in their soft, clean beds. I joined the men and their conversation about God. It took several hours, but before Mark left that night, he invited Jesus into his heart as Savior and was encouraged that, with God's help, he could get through the many problems facing him. The rain dripped off our noses as the three of us stood outside, holding hands and praying. Mark was the first of many more that Kelly and I would team-teach and tag-wrestle into the light of Christ.

The next day I came home from school and found a sign stuck in the ground by the manhole at the end of my water line. It stated that the manhole was on private property and must be moved. The meter had already been removed by the water company, consequently terminating water service. It was Dad's handy work. I had to wait until the backhoe was available, so Kelly could bring it back to dig a few feet over, removing the manhole from Dad's property and placing it suitably on county property.

Chapter Twenty-Three

In obedience to something I felt God had requested of me, I was attending church with Dad. They actually allowed me to sing solos on the platform and start a Sunday school class with my girls, Anna, and a few other little children that came for a short while. Some of the old-timers, including my Mamaw Ruth (Dad's stepmother), had a hard time accepting my beliefs and me. I knew the arrangement was short term and tried to reassure everyone of such. Kelly visited the church with us and was quite taken back by their primitive ways. On 29 October 1989, just a few miles from the church, in a cold, muddy creek about waist deep, Dad baptized the girls and me . . . it was a special and memorable event. Then a few months later God allowed us to move on.

I needed to find a church closer to home (again) and knew Garvin Ridge was out of the question. By now most of my family knew I was "Pentecostal" and tried to avoid the subject while hoping I wasn't going off the deep end. I prayed that I wouldn't spend a lot of time shopping for a church. There was a small, storefront, nondenominational church that had recently pioneered in Olive Hill. Jessica, Lacy, and I went to visit them for a Wednesday evening service. We prayed before we went in that we would know right away if that was to be our new church home and family. We timidly walked in the front door. A woman in the front row threw open her arms, shouted, "Well, praise the Lord!" and trotted over to greet us. I knew I was home.

"Two years," the Lord said. Now that I think about it, God often gives me time frames in which to operate. Not particularly in reference to *when* something will take place (now, that would be nice) but generally *after* something takes place, I have a sense of how long before His hand will again gently glide over our lives and move us into a new work. The church was called New Life Victory Church. Pastor Bob Stapleton and his wife Joyce proclaimed it as new life for the sinner and victory for the Christian. For two incredible years, I was abundantly blessed to sit at the feet of their leadership.

Joyce was a stylish, thin woman who bounced on her toes when she talked about Jesus. Her face glowed with His love, and she lavished that love on everybody that came near her. She called Jessica her "little missionary" and was awed by the sweet spirit and special calling she said the Lord had placed on Lacy. Best of all, she loved to pray, and led me into a prayer life that actually brought results. There are few people as special as Joyce Stapleton.

Brother Bob was sixty-something and the Santa Claus type. (Sorry, Brother Bob, I know you abhor "Santa Claus," but the happy, giving stereotype fits. For the reader's sake, forgive me. Okay?") Brother Bob was a man who could squeeze me in a tight hug without a speck of lust or wrongdoing. He was a plainspoken, gifted, and simple teacher behind the podium. He used a lot of stories from his past to bring out the beauty in God's Word. I'm sure I heard his "Bessie" story a dozen times.

"Bessie" was a senile, old woman from his boyhood days, that talked to herself while she walked the railroad tracks. All the kids were afraid of her, but one day Brother Bob decided to follow her (at a safe distance) to hear what on earth she was mumbling to herself over and over all day long. She had a switch cut from a willow tree and was swatting herself on the back of her legs saying, "Bessie, I told you not to go to town today. You've got work to do at home. Now you turn around and get back to the house!" She whacked her calves and proceeded toward town, thus continued the scolding. "Bessie! I *said* you get back to the house!" Swat, Swat! Finally Bessie turned around and headed back home. And that was the humorous foundation for his many teachings based on 1 Corinthians 9:27, training his flock to bring their flesh under subjection. He was also mightily anointed in the ministry of healing. He expounded repeatedly on numerous scriptures that pledge health to the body (people) of Christ. During that time my medicine cabinet was empty, not even an aspirin could be found in the house.

One morning I was at home, rushing around getting us all ready for school. I was having an unusually heavy and painful menstrual period. Then, without provocation, my nose began to bleed profusely! I don't remember *ever* having had a nosebleed, even as a child. The phone rang with Bro. Bob inquiring on the other end of the line, "Connie, the Lord told me to call you. Is something wrong?" He led me to Ezekiel 16:6 ". . . as you lay there in your blood I said to you, 'Live!' " We prayed . . . my nose stopped bleeding, the menstrual pains subsided, and I arrived at school without delay, possessing abundant ability to fulfill my day's obligations.

I like to think the Devil knew I would blossom into an impregnable, robust, hardy, etc. Christian if left unattended. Whatever his reasoning, his imps made their appearance. Around 5:00 A.M. one foggy morning, I heard music coming from the toy box in Jessica's room. She and Lacy were in bed with me, so I knew it wasn't either of them. I went to investigate. The girls had a little keyboard that was preprogrammed to play several tunes upon the press of a button. It was buried under a mound of assorted toys and was playing the song *Son of Dragon*. I pulled it out, turned it over, and removed the batteries. It shook me up a little, but I tried to shrug it off without prayer or consideration. A few days later . . . the same scenario. Early morning and noise from the toy box. I was apprehensive as I approached the strange sounds coming from the box. This time it was a doll that held batteries and normally said phrases like "I love you" and "Hi Mommy," except now her mouth was moving in slow motion and producing weird, cryptic gibberish. I nearly panicked as I pulled open the back of her frilly doll dress to remove the batteries . . . only to discover there weren't any! I threw the doll on the floor and started shouting rebukes in Jesus' name. I took authority over principalities, pleading coverage by the blood of Jesus. Immediately the attack through the doll stopped, but I continued my own attack. As a matter-of-fact, the plan backfired on the instigating wimp. I pushed through (with Bro. Bob and Joyce's help) to a whole new realm of spiritual understanding. There were no more overt attacks like that from Satan. Suffice it to say that he now tiptoes past our house, hoping *we* don't wage war against *him*! Ah, we have our battles, but he doesn't deserve credit for them.

Chapter Twenty-Four

It was Thanksgiving break and Kelly invited me to go to Kansas with him to meet his family. The girls watched nervously from Papaw and Mamaw Wanda's window as Kelly and I drove away on a snowy night. It was a quick trip, but I was a smash hit and well received by all. My first impression of Kansas was *not* favorable! I had never been that far west and wasn't aware of the engulfing magnitude of the Great Plains region. I once told Kelly how much I enjoyed the trees in Kentucky. He said, "But you can't see the sky." "What?" I was puzzled. "Of course you can see the sky. It's right there, see?" I pointed upward to the haze peering between thousands of leaves that dangled from the canopy high above. *Now* I understood what he meant. The Kansas weather was gray and cloudy the duration of our visit, as well as windy. I'm talking real wind, like constant thirty-m.p.h. wind and even stronger gusts. Kelly and I left for the return trip to Kentucky by late evening the day after the turkey feast and just as the weather began to clear. He was quiet and subdued. His soul was in the soil, for he was a tiller in his heart, and it ached for his home. We were alone on the interstate when he pulled to the side of the road. "Look," he said softly, gazing behind us. I turned around and beheld an incredible sunset! The sky was a multitude of pigments. Directly overhead, a vivid blue shifted through several shades before turning to turquoise, then purples and pinks. Even magenta and fuchsia splashed their splendor across the massive horizon. The concentric choir of colors, under the swiftly descending direction of their spherical, blazing, orange conductor, thundered hallelujahs to their audience. It was the moment Kansas greeted *my* heart and invited me to stay.

*   *   *   *   *

College moved along at a quicker pace than I cared to keep. I maintained an excellent GPA and was invited to join the Honor Society, which I declined. The main office for the elementary education program was a busy place as students paraded through, visiting advisors and tending to their typical and not-so-typical needs. During one of my visits, I noticed a newspaper clipping taped to the doorframe. It was a satiric, political cartoon with a certain state official looking bedraggled and his tongue hanging out. A voluptuous, short-skirted woman accompanied him with a caption that said something about Jack B., the womanizer. The last I heard of Jack was that his position had been dissolved, and he was suing the state for breech of contract.

Some of my classes were held in the same building that housed the university television studio. On a whim, I sauntered into the main office and asked if I could possibly observe while the programs were being taped or aired. I even volunteered to clean the studio or be a runner, anything to gain access where I could pick up knowledge in television production. The secretary told me they were short on help. She convinced me to sign up for college credit as an intern in television and radio communications. As an intern, I could work directly with the daily production. I would rotate positions with other interns, playing the roles of production room director, floor director, cameraperson, video/audio/lighting engineer, and etc. That next semester I took advantage of the opportunity. It was a lot of fun as well as informative, but it stretched my schedule too thin. One semester was enough to feed the hobby and give me valuable insight on television production. It might come in handy in the future.

Through a lady at church, I met a group called Team Thrust for the Nations. They were a group of evangelists that traveled in two scenic cruiser greyhounds witnessing on the streets about the love of Jesus. That same lady offered to pay my way if I would go to New York with her and the team for a week of street witnessing. After a lot of prayer and tripping over stumbling blocks, I decided to go. Kelly and I had been dating well over a year, and I felt it would be good for him and the girls to have some time alone. I asked him to baby-sit while I went on the trip. I was uneasy with the arrangement, but I knew I had to trust God to protect them . . . I also needed to trust people in general and realize that not everyone is out to crush others. My experience in New York was mind boggling. I could write a hundred pages telling you all the incredible things I heard and saw God perform.

There were two young men, single and new Christians, with us on that trip to New York. They took turns fighting for my attention. I was now oblivious to that sort of carrying on . . . the Spirit of God was busy teaching me and breaking my heart for His hurting people and wounded nation. What a change that was for me!

Several months after that trip, around June of 1990, Team Thrust stopped at our church while traveling through. They spent a few nights witnessing on the streets in our area. Kelly and I had been with the team on several trips after New York and had a glorious time being used by God. This time Kelly didn't want to go along, and he didn't want me to go either. One of the young men that was on the New York trip had been pursuing me with great interest and understandably, that annoyed Kelly. To me it was a lame excuse for fizzing out spiritually. I was concerned that Kelly's fervor for the Lord was going defunct. After eighteen months of dating, we weren't any closer to marriage, and I was convinced he would never have the nerve to take the plunge. More importantly, we were slipping too far into sexual temptations, and I definitely didn't want to fall into that rut again. So late in the evening, just as the katydids and frogs began to croak deep in the woods and after a summer shower left the smell of stagnant and dusty air, I broke off the relationship.

The next morning as I stepped out of the shower, there was a knock on my door. It was Kelly with roses, a fast-food breakfast sandwich, and a card. He was adorable and made my knees weak, but I wasn't ready to melt into his arms. He asked me to sit down as he knelt in front of me. He nervously handed me the card and carefully watched my expression while I opened it. It was a romantic, sweet, flowery card and had been signed with the words, "Will you please marry me?" My reaction wasn't exactly what he hoped for, but it wasn't a blunt, "No" either. I had to think about it.

Every morning that week he started showing up at dawn with my breakfast. By the third day, I finally said, "Yes," and relieved the poor guy of his patient misery. We set the date for three months later on 12 October 1990.

Kelly insisted I wear a white gown. I was his virgin bride.

Look at those expressions!

Chapter Twenty-Five

The wedding was set to take place in the middle of a school semester. I had to stay alert to keep up my grades, while arranging a wedding. I tried to convince Kelly that a simple ceremony with a justice-of-the-peace would be best, but he wanted the whole shebang! It was indeed a grand affair held at Word of Life Church where Kelly continued his attendance, after the girls and I moved to Olive Hill. There were over two-hundred guests, flowers and candles everywhere, twelve attendants, and gifts galore! Jessica was a flower girl and Lacy was a ring-bearer. They stood with us while we received prayer and took our vows. The four of us each lit a unity candle with the tallest, center candle already burning and representing Christ. We took communion together for the first time as a family. It was a magnificent wedding, as most weddings are, so I won't bore you with more of the bride's details.

Kelly's family came from Kansas and Nebraska for the big event. But sadly, a few days before her scheduled departure, Kelly's dear grandmother chose to boycott the wedding since he was marrying a divorced woman. Then his mother Delores started changing her high opinion of me and threatened to stay away as well. James (Kelly's dad) said he would be at the wedding even if Kelly were marrying a black woman (sorry, but that's what he said), and Delores could come along or not. She decided to come but proved to be a stinker the whole time. They arrived the night before the wedding and refused to visit our humble residence . . . the home where their son would soon be living with his new family. Delores never spoke to me the entire day of, or even during, the wedding. Moments before she was to be seated, she turned to Kelly and said, "It's not too late to get out of this." James and Delores refused to join-in and stubbornly sat in the sanctuary while our friends and guests crept through the receiving line giving us hugs and their blessings. After the festivity of the reception, two lines were formed surrounding the escape to our new family car that was now covered with graffiti and plastic wrap and trailing cans and streamers. Delores was posted immediately beside the exit and armed with a fist full of wheat kernels (that's the Midwestern tradition, though in Kentucky we usually threw rice at the newlyweds). Kelly and I said our good-byes to the girls, waited for them to get in place to bash us with kernels, and then we made a dive for it! As I stepped out, Delores pulled back her arm and slung the grain directly into my face with full force. The tiny pellets stung my skin, as I made my way to the car. I'm sure she intended it to hurt.

The girls were to stay with Mom, as Kelly and I left for our seven-day cruise around the West Indies. We flew out of Lexington, Kentucky, early the next morning. I had been stressed-out for weeks and was exhausted from all the excitement. Our plane was delayed due to bad weather, and there was a growing concern we might miss the cruise ship's departure. I had never flown before, so when we finally boarded the plane and took off in a thunderstorm, I was frightened. Then we broke through the clouds and leveled out in to a perfectly, clear blue sky with soft, billowing clouds below. I started crying uncontrollably. Kelly wasn't sure what to do with me, so he kept asking me to talk to him, but I wasn't able to. Between heaving sobs I finally managed to say, "This is all so beautiful." He smiled and held me while I released months, maybe years, of pent-up anxiety.

We landed in Miami and ran to our connecting flight to San Juan. Less than an hour before she pushed away from the expansive docks, we boarded a luxurious cruise ship fit for royalty. There were eight hundred passengers, but we were part of a Christian group of fifteen people and two directors. We met in the casino (while closed) for devotions and sang hymns on beautiful, white beaches with exotic surroundings. I tried my hand at snorkeling and nearly lost my bathing suit . . . and life! A doctor friend in our group was an experienced sailor, so we rented a sailboat along with he and his wife and glided out to the open Caribbean Sea. It was as though we were riding on the wings of God.

Chapter Twenty-Six

Kelly insisted on adopting Jessica and Lacy. I was pleased but concerned about what kind of havoc we might encounter when Harvey was contacted for permission. We hired a lawyer, who drafted a letter, which asked Harvey to revoke all parental rights and allow Kelly to adopt the children. In exchange he would be forgiven his child support debt, in arrears of seventeen thousand dollars! The letter was signed and returned to the lawyer without much ado. My mixed emotions were confusing to me. I was elated that my children now had a father that was willing to fight for them, as well as committing to them his life and finances. But I was dismayed that Harvey could actually give his children away. He sold his parenthood for measly money! I knew he was abominable, but this was worse than I had expected from him. I prayed that the girls didn't put together the pieces and struggle with the same emotions. Then somewhere deep in my heart, I understood Harvey did it for their good. He knew he couldn't and *wouldn't* be the father they needed and deserved. Putting aside his hate, anger, wickedness, and pain, he did the most noble, brave, and manly thing he ever did in his entire, disturbed life. Our petition for adoption was finally signed and sealed in the judges' chambers on 18 May 1992.

Our first year of marriage was quite shaky. All of us had a few things to work through, but each of us deeply wanted to be together and happy, so we diligently chipped away at the problems and stayed close to God. We attended church in Olive Hill where Bro. Bob and Joyce kept a close watch over our relationship. The girls were in the third and first grades, and I

had a year-and-a-half of school left before completion. Kelly
continued working construction, but he was never satisfied as a
wage earner.

The elderly lady that lived in the woods near us took in
one of her corrupted sons. He tried to catch my eye without
success. We suspect perhaps for revenge, he is the one who
broke into our home and robbed us four times in one year.

Earlier, in September 1991, Kelly's brother Randy announced to the family that he and his wife, Martha, felt called
to be missionaries. They would no longer be farming the family
ground with James. Come springtime, someone else would
have to take over all the farming and ranching operations. The
obvious candidate was Kelly. I was thrust into making a hard
decision that I suspected would eventually arise, but not so
quickly. During our Labor Day break, we zipped out to Kansas
for an all-family meeting.

Randy and Martha cried as they relayed all that God had
placed on their hearts. James and Delores cried because they
were scared of what the future held. I cried because everybody
else was. Pressure was applied on Kelly and me to drop our
Kentucky lives and take over the Morris post. Kelly showed
maturity as he asked hard financial questions. Delores took off
to her bedroom, bawling about how her family didn't care
about her. By the end of a grueling day, it came down to James,
Kelly, and me. It was agreed that if we took the position, the
arrangement would be the same as it was with Randy. James
would supply the equipment and land for two-thirds of the
profit. Kelly would supply all the labor for one-third. Then
after we got on our feet, James would sell out and Kelly could
run the farm on his own.

Randy and Martha owned a home close to James and
Delores but chose not to live there because of its close proxim-
ity to the in-laws. They rented it out and lived thirty miles
away. At first, Randy and Martha advised us not to live too
close to the folks. So Kelly and I made connections with a
Realtor and started house hunting from Kentucky. Randy and
Martha waffled from day to day on their plans. At one point
they even called off the entire scheme and wanted to remain as

James and Delores's partners. It was difficult to pray for guidance and a wise decision, when we weren't sure what was taking place in Kansas. I knew in reality that I didn't actually have real options. If Kelly made up his mind that he wanted to go to Kansas (and he did), then I would have to submit and support him. It was a horrendous tug-of-war in my heart, but I closed my eyes and trusted God and my husband to take good care of us. I was scared. How could I leave my family, friends, and those hills . . . oh those rich, velvety hills! Many nights I fell asleep crying and praying for God's direction and peace. Then came a dream. I was standing on the high plains of Kansas, when before me was laid out a beautiful sky. The Lord said to me, "If you will go to Kansas, I will spread out my arms every morning and surround you, to get you through the day. And every evening I will hug you again, to get you through the night." It was as though His head was the sun, and the massive sky and all its color were His arms. By February of 1992 we agreed to move to Kansas. I would give it two years, and if the girls or I didn't like it, Kelly promised the family would return to Kentucky.

In March, a month later, I discovered a lump in my breast. I had a cyst removed when I was sixteen, and everyone hoped this was equally as harmless. After several tests it was determined to be a tumor, not a cyst. Kelly was planning to leave for Kansas in April to start farming. The girls and I were to remain in Kentucky, finish the school year, and then join him in June. If the upcoming operation produced bad news, plans could be drastically changed. The doctors wasted no time whisking me into the hospital. The tumor was removed and sent to the pathologist. A few days later we breathed a sigh of relief when the report showed no sign of cancer. Thank you again, Jesus.

I had one semester of school left to complete after that spring semester. It was my student teaching semester, and after petitioning for special circumstances, the school arranged for me to complete my student teaching in Kansas as a visiting student, under the coordination of Fort Hays State University. The superintendent of the school district in which I was placed would supervise me and assign my grade, which would be posted on a FHSU transcript, and then transferred to Morehead State University for completion of my degree. It was even more complicated than it sounds.

We sold our trailer and some of the land. We kept two acres with the pond. I had worked hard on developing that land and home, and it was hard to leave it and think about establishing a new home. I valiantly fought sadness. Most of our belongings went into storage, while the girls and I alternately stayed with Mom and Dad. I don't think I would ever have made it, if the girls hadn't been so excited.

Randy and Martha decided to sell their home and approached us with a deal. They still weren't sure where they were going, but insisted they were leaving Kansas. They offered to sell the house and eight hundred acres of ranch ground for what was owed on it. We were pleased at the offer and accepted it gratefully. It was a beautiful farm with an abundant, natural water supply that formed a pond, then flowed into a creek that dried up in the summer. There were lots of tall, healthy cottonwood trees that grew along the underground spring and stood triumphantly against chaotic, torrid, and sometime arctic-like Kansas weather. The driveway wound its way down into a canyon that was green and cool. The house was small and simple. It was a beautiful place to live, and I felt compassion for Randy and Martha as they parted with it. Kelly left for Kansas in time to start the spring operations on the farm. Banks and financing institutions give young, experienced farmers incentives to start their own farm, so obtaining a loan was no problem. With no down payment and at 5 percent interest, we borrowed money to purchase the farm. Though the paperwork wasn't finished and no transfer of funds had taken place, Kelly moved into Randy and Martha's damaged house and began remodeling, working late hours after farming all day. We talked on the phone nearly every night, as he asked my opinion concerning every little detail in the house. I missed him terribly.

Chapter Twenty-Seven

After planting seven hundred acres of corn and four hundred acres of sunflowers, my husband proudly drove to Kentucky with a pickup and stock trailer to move his new family and one cat to western Kansas. The expedition was more like a three-ring circus than a smooth move, but we safely arrived at our new shelter late in the night. New carpet had been lain in the living room, so we all crashed there. At first light the phone rang. It was Delores. Already my mother-in-law was hounding us.

A family member had passed away, and his funeral was that morning at 10:00. She insisted we go. I managed to dig out dresses for the girls and myself from the boxes, as we rushed around our strange, new surroundings. The aroma of a plenteous, funeral dinner filled the large room, as I sat politely at my husband's side. Everyone talked around me, and about me while I continued smiling. My Kentucky accent quickly became a joke I grew tired of, so I opted to stay quiet as much as possible. Martha came from outside, bounding through the door carrying her eyeglasses and happily smiling. "Look!" she pointed at her glasses. At first I thought they were broken. Assuming there must be more to her enthusiasm than I understood, I waited with my pasted smile. "It's a drop of rain!" she said with pride. I thought to myself, ". . . are you exceptionally slow or what?!?" Farmers got up and rushed to the windows, others tried to look around them to see the rain cloud. I felt like I was on another planet! Kentucky averages forty to sixty inches of rain a year. In Kansas the annual rainfall averages around sixteen inches. On this particular day, the crops . . . their

livelihood . . . their life . . . were suffering from lack of mois-
ture. The prospect of rain was an exhilarating blessing from
heaven.

The closer Randy and Martha came to being missionaries
without a permanent home, the more their anxiety set in. They
started acting as though they may change their minds and want
their home back. Even though we didn't officially own the
house, we trusted their verbal commitment to the sale and
went ahead with remodeling and making permanent arrangements. Then they decided they had to have more money for
their property than originally agreed to. We pushed them for
weeks to quote a price, and they avoided us, saying they just
didn't know what God was telling them to do. Randy started
acting strangely and told other family members that we pushed
them out of their own home. Delores told others I was there to
take everything she had. Kelly was at their place a lot, working
on equipment, etc. He must have left her door open one day
because he found a note on it that said, "Shut the door, Stupid!" Another time, she stormed down our driveway and met
us on our way out. She and James had gone to look at the
fields. Kelly had used the sweeps on a field the day before and
the weeds hadn't quite died down yet. She shouted to Kelly, "Is
that the best you could do on that field!?!" She yelled about
how he wasn't working hard enough, and that they could get
somebody else to run the farm better, for less money. This kind
of haggling went on practically every day.

Randy and Martha agreed to sell their ranch for twenty
thousand dollars higher than their original quote. We decided
to get the paper work done right away, before they backed out
completely. There was a lot of hostility the day we went to sign
the papers. Randy and Martha stood back, looking at each
other with fear. I knew exactly what they were feeling. I had
also sold my home just a few months prior. They whispered
together, seemingly trying to figure a way out of the situation.
Finally, Martha grudgingly added her signature to the papers
before us, then angrily tossed the pen my way and said, "Don't
take Kelly to the cleaners."

Kelly and I argued a lot our first year in Kansas. Some of his family clearly didn't like me, and he rarely offered to defend me. Three months after we got to Kansas, my Mamaw Ruth passed away. We didn't have the money for me to fly to Kentucky for the funeral, and I would arrive too late if I tried to drive. Dad deeply wanted me to be there, so he paid for plane tickets for the girls and me to fly home. Shortly after I got back to Kansas I got Bell's Palsy, a stress-related disorder. The symptoms cleared up after a few weeks, but the stress didn't.

When autumn came, the girls started in their new school and I started student teaching in another school close to home. At first the cooperative teacher was exactly that, very cooperative and helpful. In the middle of a hot afternoon, the hired man from her farm called the school to ask if she had seen her husband. She abruptly left me with the class, in fear of where she might find him. It is common for farmers to become mangled and killed while working with the various types of dangerous, agricultural equipment, thus the alarm. When she returned, she was pale and refused to comment on her husband's whereabouts, only to say they found him, and he was all right. After that day, she was rude or despondent. It was rumored she found her husband in bed with another woman. Her husband and she soon divorced, and his lover moved in with him. That woman was the wife of the superintendent, my supervisor! Because of the terrible situation, the superintendent was understandably reluctant to come to my classroom for observations and assistance, which were necessary in order to assign me an accurate and fair grade. The cooperative teacher, due largely to her stressful and anxious circumstances, became critical and overbearing. Her teaching style was more like that of a paper-pusher . . . unlike my interactive, hands-on style. By the end of the semester, my nerves were in shambles.

It was a wonderful relief to go back east to receive my diploma and see my family. In December 1990, I graduated with a 3.25 GPA from Morehead State University, receiving a BA in Elementary Education with an emphasis in music. All my family was there and acknowledged with enthusiasm what an accomplishment I had achieved.

As I walked across the stage at my college graduation,
my daughters yelled from high up in the stadium,
"Way to go, Mom!"

Back in Kansas, none of the Morris' said or did anything
congratulatory. We had drawn names for Christmas presents
with the Morris family, and we all planned to celebrate the
holiday together once we returned from Kentucky. We got
home and discovered Randy had come into our house and got
the family presents from under our tree, then took them to the
in-laws and had Christmas without us.

After graduation I began scouting for a job. Since we live
at the corner of Kansas, Nebraska, and Colorado I obtained
teaching certificates from each state. I applied to substitute
teach in all the surrounding schools. That kept me busy and
helped with the loneliness. I had a hard time getting comfortable in the open prairie . . . I longed for the lush security of the
Appalachian hills.

A year of partnership with Kelly's parents was enough for
us. He told them he was ready to buy them out as planned.
Despite their elderly age and poor health (James has Parkinson's
Disease), they weren't ready to let go of sixty years of work and
dreams. Thus the skirmish began. Delores called an all-family

meeting in a lawyer's office. She had briefed the other three sons on how Kelly was trying to put them out of their home and leave them without an income. She tried to convince any-one of them to come run the farm, since Kelly's wife had changed everything and was out to ruin the family. All that was certainly upsetting to Kelly and me, but we knew in our hearts exactly how things had transpired. Besides farming, Kelly had also established a lucrative plumbing business, so we knew that in financial terms we would survive. Frankly though, our mar-riage and emotions were coming unraveled.

The family gathered quietly in the lawyer's office around a long, glossy, wooden table. Randy walked in with a briefcase that he never opened. The oldest son talked in silly circles, the other son declared neutrality. For the first hour, I remained quiet while the others hashed out problems that had nothing to do with the farming enterprise. I finally grew agitated and angrily took a stand. After a heated discussion, I looked at James with a plea for help. He typically stays quiet while Delores rages, but he finally spoke out against her. He said, "We *did* agree to sell out if Kelly and Connie would move out here and keep the land in the family." Delores's mouth fell open as she tried to hush him. Then she unmasked the truth when she said without thinking, "Yes, but George, *It wasn't in writing*." The meeting was over shortly thereafter.

Three months later, an estate sale took place at James and Delores's home. We bought some of the equipment, but most of it was worn out and went to other bidders. I think, in the long run, James and Delores were relieved to be free of the ongoing demands in farming. A lot of the quarrelling died down, but our relationships were still strained. Della started at-tacking my children, and that's where I drew the line. Though we lived only a few miles from them, we rarely visited. I will be there for them, come hell or high water (which I feel I've proven), but I won't stand for any more verbal abuse. That's plainly wrong.

We joined an Assembly of God Church in St. Francis, the town near where we now live. It had a small congregation and a first-time pastor that needed to improve his skills in public speaking and people relations. Besides that, he was a fairly nice guy, but a far cry from Bro. Bob. He and his wife had children the same ages as ours. As the children played and bickered together, some things were said that hurt feelings in both families. The pastor childishly cornered us several times with unfounded accusations, which originated from misunderstandings and poor communication. Once during a Sunday morning sermon, he stammered for several minutes, while prancing nervously behind the podium. He finally apologized and said "I . . . I . . . lost my thought." An elderly lady seated in the "nice, little old lady section" called out, "Well, we hope you have more than one!" She was stunned that such a slam slipped from her typically polite addresses. I tensed in embarrassment for the pastor while others snickered. We eventually decided to quietly find another church.

Kelly had been raised in the Christian Church, so that's where we went next. They immediately made him an elder and put us to work as the Youth Group leaders. That was fine with me. I loved being with energetic, young people and helping them take back things stolen or destroyed by Satan. We put a lot of energy into the group. We produced two Easter productions, which involved over a hundred teenagers each year. We started producing videos, using the kids as the talent, and then aired them on the local free-access station. It was great fun and we ministered to a variety of wounded spirits.

After two years of fund-raisers and hard work, it came time to take a spring break ski trip. We had raised enough money for everybody that wanted to go, except for two, Brady and Sharon. They were newcomers to our Youth Group and hadn't been a part of the fund-raisers, and therefore didn't have the money to make the trip. They were "going out" with each other, and for various reasons I really wanted to see them go. Not only were we going to snow ski, but we were also going to Marilyn Hickey Ministries in Denver, Colorado, for church meetings and to see THE TOYMAKER—a fantastic production about God, the toymaker, and how the bad guy, Satan, goes around destroying all His toys. The toys are God's creation and represent humanity. So Kelly and I paid their way, two hundred fifty dollars each, to go with us.

We rented a tri-level condominium with a fireplace and an *almost-outside*, public whirlpool. After a glorious day of skiing the teens were piled on the couch resting. Brady and Sharon were snuggled close as she pretended to be falling asleep, which caused her head to slide down his chest and come to rest on his lap with her face buried in his groin area. I gritted my teeth and waited for the right words to come to me. The other kids were teasing them so much that she finally started giggling and slid off onto the floor. A little later some of the teenagers, including my Jessica and Brady and Sharon, decided to hit the whirlpool. I was helping in the kitchen when one of the older girls came in and said the kids were behaving inappropriately in the whirl-pool. She said they were acting nasty with some boys from Mississippi and using dirty language. I asked if Jessica was one of them. She wouldn't answer, which convinced me of her guilt. My temper hit the roof! About that time, Jessica walked in with a towel wrapped around her bathing suit and steaming from the winter air against her hot body. I screamed at her to go upstairs and get dressed. *My anger was a mistake.* Then Brady and Sharon came in, laughing mischievously, unwrapped and hanging limp around each others' body. I was a little calmer, but not much, as I told them to get dressed and prepare for dinner.

There were eleven teenagers quietly gathered around the table and living room. Dinner was over, and it was time to talk about what happened. I began by apologizing for losing my temper. I told them I was disappointed in the report I got and should have handled it much differently. We took turns shar-ing our thoughts and ideas on the situation, what was done wrong, and how each of us could have done it better. The initial incident wasn't nearly as roguish as I had feared. They were great! I was proud to be with them and told them how glad I was to be a part of their spiritual journey with Christ.

Then, having never before mentioned my past in public, I started opening up about my life and some of the things I had been through. I vaguely told them of the incest I endured at the hand of my stepfather. I chose to expose and give away a precious part of my soul as I haltingly shared with them how "my wakeup call was his finger in my vagina." They weren't shocked, they hear that kind of language every day. I explained that I wanted desperately to protect them from the same scars and memories that try to plague my life. They could see my heart as I begged them to preserve themselves till marriage. It opened a new door of trust, like perhaps I wasn't the goody-goody they thought I was. They too shared some of their ugly stories. We cried and hugged until after midnight. After the healing took place and a sweet spirit rested upon each of us, we divided up and headed to bed.

After the others were out of sight, Brady asked if he could talk to me. He thanked me for caring and helping to protect him. He talked at length about a past sexual relationship and how he wanted to be a better person. I told him again that I was wrong for yelling. We laughed when he said, "That's okay, my Mom yells at me all the time." So his heart was clear, and I made my way to my bed. Just as I got to the stairs that led to the third level, one of the girls whispered my name to get my attention. She wondered if she could talk to me. We sat on the steps, and I held her hands and listened as she told of how she's often tempted to commit suicide. I felt completely inadequate, but willing and hoping to shed light on her darkness. Sometime in the early morning hours, I found my assigned spot on the floor and lay down with a heart swollen full of joy and meekness. I was elated to be right where God wanted me.

The rest of the week was fabulous. Brady and Sharon behaved as Christians should, and the church services were right on target. Back in Kansas the trip was given high marks and praise at church and home. A few weeks passed, then the rumor mill started cranking out some troublesome tales. Stay awake, this gets tangled up.

One of the girls that cried the most that night in the condo talked to her mother about what happened. Her mother talked to Sharon's mother, who talked to my neighbor and so-called friend, who convinced Sharon's mother to talk to my pastor about my behavior on the trip. None of these people attended our church, and despite their wagging tongues and pigheaded opinions, sadly, all claimed to be Christians.

Two of our youth group "kids" surprised me with a kiss during a
pantomime performance . . . I later got a pie in my face!

Our Pastor was an overconfident, young, family man who
had changed his name from Jose to John. He spoke openly of
taking medication for a chemical imbalance, which caused him
to be temperamental and overemotional. Though our church
was his first to pastor, we enjoyed his teaching style and found
him knowledgeable and approachable. Pastor John, without
talking to Kelly and me, called a meeting with his Pastoral
Relations Committee, who decided that Kelly and I must be
ousted as Youth Leaders immediately before we procured any
more damage.

The next day was Sunday and Pastor John asked us to
come into his office after church. It was then he dropped the
bombshell. We were shocked! He said it wasn't my angry out-
burst that was the problem. It was the "vagina" word that had
"a lot" of parents upset. We were to tell the youth group *that*
night that we would no longer be their leaders. Pastor John and
two of the committee members would also be there to make
sure we minded our P's and Q's as we told the teenagers the
news.

The normal Youth Group time arrived, and one of the mothers who supported us also came. Most of the kids had already heard what was happening and came to the meeting to defend us. In marched Pastor John and two sour-faced, female, Pastoral Relations Committee members. Kelly opened with prayer and gave me the floor. I asked the kids if they remembered us talking about having to pay for mistakes. They said they did. "And remember," I cautiously continued, "that sometimes mistakes cost a huge price, and other times the cost is minor." They sat motionless; one of the girls was already crying. "Well, my mistake on the ski trip has cost me a huge price. It means I will no longer get to spend time with you as your leader." The kids had been hearing the gossip, but they wanted to know exactly what happened. I wasn't really clear about the central complaint, so the scene turned to Pastor John and his staunch brigade. He was the bad guy in the eyes of the teenagers, and he felt it, so he backed out of responsibility and left more questions hanging. I told them people were upset with me for sharing the story of my abuse. When I said they were particularly upset that I used the word "vagina," a mother in attendance shot up her hand. "Excuse me!" She was angry, and I had hoped that anger wouldn't crop up. She continued ". . . but God made those!" I laughed and decided it was over, even though the majority in the room wanted to fight to keep us.

That week Kelly requested a meeting with the Pastoral Relations Committee. He wanted to know what was told and how this got so blown out of proportion. The meeting was heart wrenching. I stared at the floor in disbelief, wiping constant tears as they went over the accusations. I considered myself fortunate that they didn't try to bring court charges against us. I was so torn from the stubborn ignorance in that room that my heart began to break. The pastor nodded his head in agreement when I cried and said I was nothing but a wretched sinner . . . then he stopped short as I finished my sentence . . . "but I know God loves me and forgives me and can use me to reach these young people." Kelly was angry and wanted concrete answers, which they couldn't give, because, in all honesty, the fuss wasn't over the ski trip or my candidness. That was a decoy. The real issue was more about a small band of people who insisted on retaining power and authority over the church and pastor. Kelly and my charismatic natures were not conducive to their *religious* agenda. Poor John was duped and didn't even know it, at least not until it was too late.

Chapter Twenty-Eight

In the summer of 1996, I got an airline ticket to Kentucky on sale for ninety-nine dollars roundtrip. I was extremely depressed, on Prozac, and still coming unglued. I'd like to go into detail here concerning depression, but it's better I leave that to the professionals. I can, however, speak with authority when I say it's a dark, dark, state of being. It was unshakable for me. I couldn't smile, think . . . or exist. I sat at my kitchen table staring at the endless rolling pasture just outside the glass doors and beyond my patio . . . I pondered how to kill myself. I figured a gun to my head was the way, but (now it's almost comical) I was too tired to figure out how to load it. At that moment, I knew for my children's sake, I had to do something. I called the airlines and discovered the cut rate. God's mercy is never ceasing.

On the plane, I was reading a book about overcoming depression through Scriptures. The author had also included a knowledgeable explanation for the physiological causes of depression. Somewhere between Chicago and Columbus, high in the air, this book was birthed. I had thought many times about writing my autobiography but put it off. I spent that week visiting family and scribbling the outline of my life. The night before I was to return home, I was able to worship the Lord with Bro. Bob and Joyce and my old friends at New Life Victory Church. It was an awesome time in the Lord. I knelt at the altar and shivered under the power and anointing of the Holy Spirit. Others were long gone, but Bob and Joyce stayed in prayer until the Lord was finished with me. Like King David, I arose with the proclamation, "My heart is fixed!"

In June, Kelly and I knew that if we were going to be in a spirit-filled church . . . where the Word of God was taught to "real" people with "real" problems and where the Holy Spirit was allowed to move, touch, and heal . . . then it was going to take a sacrifice. At the time, we felt there were no such churches in St. Francis. The closest Pentecostal/Charismatic denomination was thirty miles away, so we went to check it out.

Pastor Ross Goodman and his wife Rose Ann were gracious. They and several others sensed we were hurting and asked to anoint us and pray for us. They gathered around Kelly and me and gently lay their hands on our shoulders and top of our heads as they sought the Lord concerning our spiritual health. Our girls were ages twelve and fourteen and fit in beautifully with the dynamic youth group that was going forward like a freight train in the things of God. Jessica and Lacy were ready to jump on board and say, "Here I am Lord, I'm a little ravaged from battle. Can You do anything with me?" I made sure I told Pastor Ross and Rose Ann fragments of my past before we made a decision to stay. I was curious to see if they could handle my character and the way it had been formed. If they preferred pristine parishioners, it was better to find out right away. They were coolly unconcerned about our pasts, interested instead in where we were in our walk with God at present and, more pointedly, excited to hear where we wanted to go with God.

In the six years preceding our membership at Calvary Gospel Church in Goodland, Kansas, the Lord had shown me I was on a wilderness journey. Many beautiful lessons sprung forth into my spirit from those few words. If I could pick only one to share it would be the concept of an oasis. I think God allowed my spirit to become parched and thirsty for a mere sip of His presence. For when It came, It was sweet beyond words. . . . God, His Holy Spirit, His embrace, His Son on the cross dripping blood, my dry and black ashes turned into beauty, my clothed nakedness, the gentle breeze as He brushes by, the peaceful swaying of deep rooted love, the rest found in cool shade while protected from the hot, scorching heat of the world . . . these things are found at "The Oasis."

Revival broke out in our church a few months after we arrived. I wasn't really expecting it and (ashamedly) sure wasn't praying for it, but God gave it anyway. People reserved by nature were confessing sins and dancing with their whole heart to music that gave Jesus honor. Pastor Ross sobbed behind the podium as he apologized to the church for not leading them to the Lord as well as he could have. Tall, elegant, and impeccably-dressed Rose Ann gave all she had to worshipping her Savior and being nurtured to a closer walk with Him. People were slain in the Spirit from front to back and in between. At first, I was too cold to reach out for the blanket. It was easier to remain snuggled up in my safe, protective world in which I had enveloped myself for thirty-four years. I was sitting in my pew, feeling lifeless and unmoved, as I watched miracles take place around me. The speaker, Mike Taylor, asked everyone to come to the front, take a piece of paper from the basket he provided, and write what we wanted most from God. I went forward like all good little Christians should, took the paper and pencil, and knelt on the floor with the others. I considered what to write. I thought I should ask for my children to be mighty Christians, or for a wonderful marriage . . . I was trying to keep it down to something manageable by God. Out of the blue, I thought of writing, "I wish I had never been abused and raped." Time ran out, so I jotted down exactly that, tossed it back with scoff into the basket, and returned to my seat. A few moments later, while the worship team led us in songs of adoration, the Spirit of the Lord said to me, "I want you to thank me that you were abused." Had He been a human, I might have slapped Him! How dare He make such a request! . . . But I knew the moment was mine to grab, if only I had the nerve. Where I could hide from view, I went to the end of my pew and knelt in the narrow walkway next to the wall. At the time, I didn't understand God's request. I told Him I would receive His healing, but could it please be private. I didn't want to hop, holler and hoot, or foam at the mouth like a demon-delivered deviant. That seemed to turn off the flow of the Lord, so I got up and went to the back of the church to wait for my family. They were all kneeling at the altar, taking care

of their own business with the Lord. The exit to the sanctuary
was in the back, with an overflow section positioned close by.
I sat in the front pew of the added wing with my Bible and
purse in tow, ready to make a quick getaway. Reflecting upon
this reminds me how Satan slowly undermines our footing, so
we're unaware of an imminent, disastrous fall. I teetered on
that tragic edge. I'm ashamed I allowed myself to entertain
such a cold attitude. Two ladies started walking toward me,
each coming from opposite directions. I knew I was had! They
sat on each side of me and started praying for me. Before long
the Lord permeated my hardness.

I realized I had hatred in my spirit toward preachers and,
unknown to him, Pastor Ross deserved my apology. I asked
one of the ladies to find him and have him come talk to me
(there was a lot of commotion going on in the sanctuary at the
time . . . maybe twenty bodies lying prostrate on the floor, people
running, shouting, praying loudly and weeping . . . weeping . . .
weeping . . .). Ross made his way to where I sat, and I boo-
hooed an explanation and apology that probably made no sense,
but it was done nonetheless. He hugged me cautiously and
commenced to pray over me, as did the ladies. I doubled over
in my seat, holding my stomach from gut-wrenching rips. I
wailed like an angry toddler, not caring how I looked or how
loud I carried on. The Lord pulled away heartache after heartache, until I finally screamed in agony. That brought others to
the scene. I prayed my children weren't watching, but if they
were would God please help them understand.

People were praying feverishly and making me wonder if I
could take any more "healing." I thought about saying, "That's
all folks. I've gone as far as I care to go. Stop praying now. I
can't endure any more." But I yearned to be free of the cloud
that loomed over me all my life. I was afraid if I pushed God
away this time, He may never make the same offer again, so I
continued with the process . . . it wasn't near being over. I leaned
over the lap of a lady next to me, then felt as though I might
vomit. I *did* pull back at that moment and asked God to please
not list regurgitation as a requirement in this course. With no
waste can in sight, I thought of the nice, red carpet and decided

to lie down on the floor. The nausea passed, and in rushed mighty, boisterous waves of cleansing. It started at my feet and moved up my perspiring body to the top of my head in vibrations that came again and again. Every speck of my body took turns tensing and releasing in sweet shivers. As my legs quit trembling and the river flowed against gravity up my body, my back arced and breathing ceased . . . I remembered the beatings, burnings, vile touches and words . . . my teeth even chattered as the river flowed through my mouth, cleansing my own fowl utterances. Then a few seconds of rest before it came again, beginning with my toes . . . the ones my mother used to kiss . . . then up and out. I visualized a maze so intricate that no mastermind could conquer it, yet here was the Holy Spirit weaving in and out with superior intelligence, knowing exactly what turn to take, erasing hidden secrets, and illuminating dark corners before exiting . . . then swiftly returning to another concealed passageway.

I'm guessing I was on the floor several hours. I could have stopped it at any time, because I wasn't in a trance or outside of my body. I was fully aware of my actions, yet totally uninvolved in causing them. I made myself allow God complete control . . . well, that's not exactly true . . . I *could have* flopped like a fish there on the floor. I worked hard at holding my bones together as they rattled. Ezekiel 37:1-14 captures the idea better than I, ". . . can these (dry) bones live? . . . Oh Sovereign Lord, you alone know." In that passage, with a rattling sound, the Lord pieced together dry bones and recreated a breathing being . . . as He did in me.

My husband always finds the humor in things. Even if it doesn't exist, he creates it! He particularly found it amusing how God caused this scene of deliverance to take place right in front of the main exit from the sanctuary. As people left the church that night, they had to either walk around me or over me, thus blowing my plan to be discreet.

God is a different person to me today than He was this time last year, as I suspect He will be this time next year. My prayer time has increased from fifteen minutes a day to an hour a day, and that is not nearly enough. I could spend countless hours studying the Bible, only to open more doors to God's plan through which I must explore.

Chapter Twenty-Nine

After substitute teaching for three years, I was hired as the first grade teacher in a rural school where I have taught for five years. I love the students from my heart, while educating them with enthusiasm and creativity. It's been difficult at times to accept that there are children I will be unable to rescue. Some of them come from destitute home-lives that would break the hardest of hearts.

The daily neglect, abuse, hunger, filth, and parental apathy in which many of our nation's children live is unforgivable. Teachers are required to perform far beyond their training, often forfeiting their own time and money to augment education, many times risking their lives for the sake of others: all for an embarrassing salary! Test scores continue to decline while violence among and against students increases. Society seems to have placed little emphasis on the value of educating our youth, a message sent by shallow funding for needed supplies and equipment. Attendance centers are often rubbled structures, appearing more formidable than inviting and interesting.

Despite my complaints, academia has an energy that enlivens me. With an imperative nature, somewhat driven by the groans of the common soul of humanity, I am committed to working with others to find effective rejoinders to befuddled issues such as these. Being an advocate for the child, I have many times fought parents and the system for their benefit. That's certainly one of the least pleasurable tasks as an educator.

Lewis was an adorable, but troubled youngster. It was the end of the year, and I made arrangements for a field trip to a local tourist attraction. The students needed no money for the event, just a packed lunch and drink. Lewis lived along the route to the site, so it was arranged to pick him up on our way there. The bus pulled in front of his tattered, mobile home. After a brief wait, the driver blew the horn. The front door bolted open and out burst Lewis! His dirty little hands and face, disheveled clothing, and uncombed hair made it obvious he had just climbed from bed. He was so excited for the trip that his motorized feet stumbled over each other and sent him plummeting to the ground. He barely touched the ground as he caught himself, bounced up, and proceeded to run for his ride. In one hand swung a plastic bread bag, which I assumed was his lunch. Lewis plopped down beside me, and the bus pulled out. A few minutes later, Lewis started rummaging through his bag for something to eat. I had to remind him that eating was not allowed on the bus.

"Just one biscuit?" He asked as he held up the miniature baked good as though I should inspect it for approval, "I ain't had no breakfast."

My heart ached as I helped him put away the biscuit. I wasn't upset over his missed meal, that was an everyday occurrence for many of my pupils. But the biscuit . . . was hard! And his "bagged lunch" contained six more cold, hard biscuits, with nothing else. Nothing! Evidently his mother hadn't prepared his lunch, and on the way out the door he grabbed the stale bag of yesterday's biscuits for his breakfast *and* lunch.

The sadness goes, but is never ceasing. It's not uncommon for a child to arrive at school wearing the same clothing from the day *or days* before, often stained with dribblings from the school lunches, perhaps their single, daily meal, or reeking of a foul urine stench. I've had to comfort and support a little girl after being examined by a physician to prove or disprove reports of sexual molestation by her caregiver. The results, by the way, were inconclusive.

Once during recess duty, a young boy with a plaster cast on his hand and forearm, drew back his fist to strike me after

I dismantled a fight he had provoked. Challenging him with unswerving boldness made him back down. Another dangerous incident occurred when a group of delinquent high school boys surrounded me with lust in their eyes and vulgar, sexual innuendoes seeping through the talk that attempted to entrap me. Growing bored of the threat, without flinching, I began speaking to them in tongues as though I was carrying on a conversation. It completely disarmed the leader! He was speechless as the others burst out laughing at his dumbfounded expression. "You're crazy man!" they said, as I tossed back my head, smiled in agreement, and nudged my way through the gang.

My experiences in the classroom have brought me joy, as well as great sorrow. I've recorded numerous anecdotes that I will treasure forever, an adored one being the time I asked my first graders what was a "manger" and a student answered, "It's a hay bowl!"

Reviewing our Thanksgiving lessons, I hoped my students could recall the name Squanto, who befriended the pilgrims and was part of the Massasoit Tribe, of which Samoset was the Chief. After my initial inquiry, the class searched their young minds for an answer to please the teacher they loved so dearly. Then from the silence came the brilliant response that made us *all* laugh . . . "Samo-squat!"

I love telling stories when I teach. The kids say they like to hear me talk (rumor has it that teachers like to hear *themselves* talk). Maintaining a bit of my southern accent makes my country stories fun to tell. As a prank, I asked the kids if they heard about the hillbilly that got fired from the M&M factory? Perhaps I was laying the foundation for a lesson on community workers, I don't know, but whatever the case, they fell for it. "Why?" They asked with worry for the fired factory worker. I kept a straight face, "Because she kept eating the W's!" No response, I waited; still, they didn't get it. Guilt tugged at my conscience when I realized they were sincerely concerned for this worker. I quickly attempted an explanation, even drawing an illustration on the board to point out the humor, but it was too late. Their minds were swirling with questions, and I had lost the class. "She got *fired*!?!" . . . "Why was the boss so mad?" . . . The kids blasted away with innocent outrage and curiosity. It was one of those "teaching moments" that quickly fell apart, but did finally provide a great laugh.

In the Bible, John 2:1-11 tells of Jesus turning water into wine. Before that miracle could take place, the servants had to fill the pots with the water. That's my job. I have thoroughly enjoyed *filling* those "wonderfully and fearfully created" vessels, then it's up to the Spirit of God to turn common knowledge into a wealth of opportunities and wonderful experiences. Most likely, the servants at that Cana wedding never got to enjoy the wine for themselves, just as teachers seldom experience the manifested richness of *their* efforts. Sure, we teachers are privileged to spend with our students some precious moments, but once that child leaves the teacher's tutorage, their success is up for grabs by many greedy takers. The real influences in a child's life come from home . . . and there lies the root of responsibility for all a child learns. *Education begins and ends at home.*

I've been involved in a lot of ministries, led sitter-cise classes in a nursing home, a jail ministry for two years, taught Sunday school for seven years, and currently acting as "head chef" for our Sunday morning children's breakfast program. Sometimes the Lord allows me to minister before the congregation or pray with others during the altar service. Beautiful transformations unfold at the altar as the river of God rushes through. Unforgettable was the expression of a young man with blue hair seeking the Lord at the altar. His hair protruded in straight, stiff, sharp spikes as he chomped on chewing gum and stood in the prayer line with his hands in his pockets and without emotion. I walked over to him, softly placed my hand on his forehead, and waited silently for the Lord to direct my praying. I opened my eyes, looked directly into the young man's eyes, and asked him to spit out his gum into my hand, which I held politely beneath his chin. He obliged. Without hesitation, I threw the gum in my mouth and began to chew! The boy was shocked and now very attentive. I calmly stated how God wants to "swallow up everything that troubles you." Instantly, the young man was able to press through, finding God passionately waiting to meet with him.

Yet, I find it most rewarding intermingling the gospel with everyday business, which seems to be a real challenge for many of us. It's fun to see the surprise and interest in the eyes of unchurched or unkept 6-year-olds, when I exclaim, "Wow! Praise God!" over their scribbled accomplishments. Or better yet, the look of dismay from my *reportedly* homosexual principal when I boldly praise God in his presence.

I carpool a seventy-mile commute with Lucille Rossbach, a Lutheran pastor's wife, an English teacher, and poet. She and I laugh a lot, even cry sometimes, and pray for the needs of our students, family, and friends. Seeing the need for prayer in our school, I opened my classroom for a five-minute, morning-prayer session for anyone that wanted to attend. The custodians and one of the cooks showed up a few times, other than that, in two years, sadly, no one else answered the urge to attend. I pray

I cherish being in the classroom.

that America's educators, politicians, and church and social leaders of all walks of life, being equipped and empowered to make a difference in society's ills, will know how to embrace with understanding and contest with astute fervor the wrongs in our world . . . I believe it begins with prayer.

Chapter Thirty

Kelly and I enjoy a strong marriage and wonderfully, precious relationship. We are more in love and happier than ever before. He's a gift to me from God. While writing this book, his shoulders bore the brunt of my anguish.

As I prepared breakfast at church for the Sunday School children, Kelly taught the adult class and shared each week with our friends the progress of my work. Their support was important to him as he solicited their prayers for both of us. The bruising experience of my precarious memories floundering to the surface and going to print was difficult for everyone in our home. My mood was sober and silent for many weeks as the first half of this work emerged. Relief echoed throughout the household upon completion of the passage that relayed my salvation, a turning point in my life *and current disposition.* Kelly entered his Sunday School classroom, smiling broadly with transparent pleasure and eagerly announced, "Shew! She finally got saved!"

My husband was the first to read the preceding chapters in this book and approve its continuance. I trusted his decision to put it in the hands of our children for reading. Had he disapproved, I would have hidden it away from human eyes, leaving it only for my girls to read much later in life. Not only did he approve, he seemed proud of me *and* was sad for me. He urged me on, as I lumbered through memories I preferred to leave forgotten.

A farmer, rancher, and part-time plumber, Kelly takes great pride in supplying the world with the bread of life, both physically and spiritually. Agriculture is his baby . . . he studies and analyzes it . . . he prays over seed as it goes in the ground and stands before his fields awe struck at God's provision to His people. He's a man of the earth . . . loves the creator and tenderly cares for all creation . . . from stubborn steers to stubborn sinners.

Though numbed by the financial hazards involved in agriculture and raising livestock, my husband and I find the spirit of the occupation rewarding. I am an integral part of all operations on our farm and ranch, which includes fifteen hundred acres of crop ground and twelve hundred acres of rangeland for grazing cattle. I pray I'll be allowed to grow old here, with my husband, as we rock in our porch swing, holding hands, and beholding the beauty of our lives together in western Kansas.

Jessica and Lacy are busy about the Lord's business. They each work hard at daily chores, but of utmost importance, they're into God's Word daily and vigorously reaching for an ever-increasing, alive relationship with Jesus. I'm a strict mother, sometimes overbearing, but it seems necessary as we evolve through life. My prayer for them, if they choose to marry, is to receive their first kiss at the wedding altar. I say that with a serious, slow smile. Make it or not, I'll always continue to be proud of them. They were the second critics of this autobiography. Had they been uncomfortable with any part of it, it would have been removed. Had they requested it go no farther, it wouldn't have. Jessica jokingly said she didn't think she would want it in the high school library. Lacy cried through a few passages, and we had a sweet moment of sharing concerning some of the harsh content.

After my family read this story, I sent it to Brother Bob and Joyce and Pastor Ross and Rose Ann for review. I had asked both pastors to double-check my comments on Scriptures, as well as how they felt in general concerning the content. Brother Bob and Joyce both read it in a week and called with enthusiasm.

"So, you think it's all right?" I asked hesitantly. "Publish that thing, girl!" were Brother Bob's words. Both he and Joyce were on the line at the same time, bubbling over with joy and excitement for me and the ministry in front of this disclosure.

Pastor Ross submitted to Rose Ann's request to read this book first. She was aware of the general topic and wanted to make sure there wasn't "anything that would hinder my pastor from ministering to me." After five weeks, on a Sunday morning, I was in the church kitchen, when Pastor Ross handed over my manuscript with a four-page, typed letter from Rose Ann. She asked the pastor, her husband, not to read it. She told me, ". . . you might as well put a pornographic magazine in (his) hands!" At one point, with an accusing, sharp tone, she glared at me saying, "Why would you want to do this"?

It is this "churched" mentality that prevents hundreds of hurting hearts from coming to Christ for the compassion and healing He so longingly wishes to bestow upon his battered children. If you are one of these, take heart! Remember that others are working through their own crippled thinking, perhaps even their own experiences with abuse. It's the sovereignty of God to utilize His people in an anointed area of ministry, yet, at the same time, tolerate that servant's lack of knowledge in other areas. The answer: Just hang on to good old-fashioned love for one another, even for the most stubborn and ignorant of all. And don't forget to keep laughing and living!

After Rose Ann and I avoided each other for several weeks, we had a long talk and were finally able to relinquish control of the issue to the Spirit of God. We have since continued to flourish in Christ, together.

Next to review this book, were my parents, brother, and sisters. They weren't particularly upset with me. Mom and I cried together on the telephone, and she expressed that she finally felt, like the song, that her burdens had been washed away. But several weeks later, I received a letter from her in which she shamed me for writing and *thinking* such terrible things, especially about the family.

Dad has yet to make any comment. I respect his need to weigh and process these printed words privately.

*   *   *   *   *

Kelly's family seems to have accepted me, at least on the surface. Randy apologized for the hurt he caused us and is working with the Lord in Denver, Colorado, along with his wife and four children. It's fun to get together and relish the grandeur of Christ together.

My Dad and Wanda divorced bitterly. A couple of years later, Dad suffered a mild, but somewhat crippling stroke. He sold the church, and he and the members are in a legal scuffle over the proceeds.

Anna was in college for a while, but dropped out and married her high school sweetheart. They have a quiet and sweet life, but I'm unsure of their relationship with Christ.

My mother is still married to her third husband, Roy Mabry, and seems to be happily settled in the marriage. They still go to church at Garvin Ridge and worship the Lord in their own way. She and I are friends, but our relationship is strained and awkward. Last Christmas, while I was visiting my family in Kentucky, in the middle of a lighthearted conversation, Mom said to me, ". . . Of all your education, you still turned out to be a nobody" . . . Oh well, that's my Mother and I love her dearly!

Cindy recently divorced her third husband for horrible reasons that aren't mine to share. As she read this book she said, "(she) cried right along with me."

Billy divorced last summer after tiring of his wife's substance abuse and marital unfaithfulness. He has remarried and is soon to be a grandfather. After reading the first two drafted chapters of this book, he refused to finish, stating he ". . . didn't have the interest . . ."

Harvey remains an alcoholic and drug addict. He's a frequent inmate of the county jail, his charges ranging in severity from public intoxication to attempted murder. He never calls for holidays or birthdays, but I encourage my daughters to keep in touch with him.

Damion B., the last I heard, is lost in sin and continues chasing young girls for his pets.

Remember Pastor John and the Assembly of God pastor? Both humbly apologized for the way our work in their church fell apart and have sought to rebuild our friendships. My family and I respect and appreciate both of them. We count them as brothers.

In 1991 I saw Don Clark hobbling down the sidewalk like a beggar. His clothes and shoes were ragged. Determined to seize a moment for which God had been preparing in my heart for many years, I called his name and ran to catch up to him. Out of breath and observing his puzzled expression, I said, "It's Connie. How are you?" He said, "Connie, I . . . I . . . Connie . . . Hi . . . It's good to see you!" He paused for the slightest of breath, as he seemed to study me in disbelief. Then he stammered on, but with surety ". . . I'm . . . I'm sorry for . . . you know . . . I'm sorry." I smiled and said, "It's okay. I wanted to catch you to tell you I forgive you." I told him I was able to love him with God's love, and I hoped the best for him. He touched my hand and smiled the same compassionate smile I had seen him use against me hundreds of times. I pulled away and said good bye. I heard he died not long after that.

It was that incident on the street that sunny day, with the perpetrator of my incest, that revealed to me the precious love and forgiveness of God. It was a divine appointment for both of us. I needed to express forgiveness. That's just simply God's way. He, my stepfather, needed to say he was sorry. It seemed the words were on the tip of his tongue, and *had been* for years. They just fell out. Without forethought, or effort, the words that had worn him out, reduced him to a street bum, and destroyed his health . . . tumbled into existence and set him free. I wouldn't be surprised to see him in heaven.

If God could love Don Clark and make a way, on the eve of his death, for him to be released from the chains that bound him for years, receive forgiveness, and get closer to heaven, then God could surely love me and forgive me too. The arms of Jesus, once stretched against the splinters of His sacrifice for us . . . now . . . in His strength . . . embracing at the same pivotal moment . . . *the abused and abuser*. With confounded and tearful appreciation, acknowledging my inadequacy as an author, I ache to express how expansive is the love of Christ. I pray you already know, or you are soon to understand.

Chapter Thirty-One

I wrote this book because I believe God asked me to. It's really that simple and could be left at that. However I can enumerate the reasons shown to me.

First, it was for my children and husband. They knew bits and pieces of my life, but the details were too vulgar to discuss. I believe putting it in the form of a descriptive story helps answer the questions too personal to ask. It's okay if you disagree with that ideal. Time will either prove or disprove the theory.

Second, it was for you. Ut-oh, I just heard someone huff and puff with righteous indignation. Okay, maybe it had nothing to do with you. I know parts of it were private and invasive, I apologize if you feel you've been defiled.

But for you who cried, or sensed the Holy Spirit nudging you along the way for whatever reasons . . . I stuck my neck out for you . . . and you are worth it! By the way . . . I am glad I was abused . . . *I thank God I was abused* (See Ephesians 5:20) . . . so I could become who I am and write this for you.

Third, it seems possible that God may be leading me into a public life, perhaps in the position of a political official. It's not somewhere my flesh wants to go, but if the Lord wants me there, I'm willing . . . No! . . . I'm thrilled to go! This story needed to be told before I got there . . . I'm sure you understand why.

Fourth and last, if for no other reason, I have to believe this was a catharsis for me. I'm not yet convinced it was, but maybe that will come later. It took six years to struggle through it. Many times I had to stop, fall on the floor, and cry out to

God to remind me again why I was doing this. My heart pounded as I approached my writing center. Sometimes I broke out in a sweat and with labored breathing as I wrestled for the right words and courage to print them. It wasn't a flippant idea or spur of the moment brainstorm. It wasn't fun, but Jesus sat next to me hour after hour and soothingly reassured me it would be all right.

Chapter Thirty-Two

It seems God has put a new vision in my heart. I've been consumed with a burden for our nation and the people of America. Actually, all over this earth are people like you and me that need breath blown into our dry bones. Indifference has put us asleep.

I searched God's Word for proof that it is appropriate for a woman, mother, wife, and plain-ole country girl to seek a role in secular and political leadership. Astounded at how I had overlooked it for years, I discovered public policy and security of His people is the heartbeat of Christ!

Consider chapter four of Judges. Mentioned immediately in verse four is the status of Deborah, a prophetess, wife, and leader of the nation of Israel. She foretells ". . . the Lord will hand Sisera [the enemy] over to a woman" . . . and that woman was a tent-dweller, a woman of the open air and country, named Jael, also a common housewife. I join in the tolls of Deborah's song, chapter five, and cling to the concluding verse: "So may all your enemies perish, O Lord! But may they who love you be like the sun when it rises in its strength. Then the land had peace forty years." Fear taunts me as I'm often convinced I will be swallowed alive by the sharks in the tank of public service. This will be one of the banner prayers of my heart: that God's enemies will perish; that I and others who love the Lord shall rise in strength; *and* . . . I'm feeling rather audacious for speaking it . . . under my leadership the people may experience peace for forty years!

Repeatedly searching my heart for God's assurance that His anointing of political leadership indeed rests upon me has

taken me through many scriptures. Psalm 12:2 "Everyone lies
to his neighbor, their flattering lips speak with deception."
Then further on in the same chapter, Verse six, ". . . the words
of the Lord are flawless, like silver refined in a furnace of clay,
purified seven times." The plea of my existence in politics is
that I may speak as would please the Lord, with no careless
words, but rather with purest truth, without flattery, deceit,
and lies. It is imperative to me that I do service for God's
creation in this manner. I am not entering politics so my dis-
trict/state/nation may become greater, but rather, to lead many
to Christ, so the population of Heaven will be greater because
of me. My past has established within me conviction and
tenacity . . . now I am compelled . . . I am *empowered* to fight
for others.

Finding Daniel 4:17b rooted and grounded the validity of
God's call in my heart and spirit to enter the hallowed chambers of legislative action:

*   *   *   *   *

*The Most High is sovereign over the kingdoms of
men and gives them to anyone he wishes and sets
over them the lowliest of men. (Dan. 4:17b)*

*   *   *   *   *

America is in trouble. You know it, don't you? Oh, there
are days I sit back with a deep sigh, gaze naively into the clear
blue sky, and feel nothing can touch me. An alarmist I may be.
A Christian enthusiast . . . I hope so! The leaders of our country need your prayers in mighty ways. We need to get out of
ourselves and into the mind of God. I'm not prepared to talk
politics beyond this . . . *We need Jesus.* . . . Too simplistic in a
complicated system of government? . . . Too idealistic in a society gone askew? Too wimpy against the evil that's raging
from high places to the filthiest ghetto? Check out Zechariah
4:6, ". . . Not by might, nor by power, but by My Spirit, says
the Lord Almighty."

Our home is situated in the middle of the pasture on our
ranch. We have a fence surrounding the home with two cattle

guards for entry. It's peaceful watching the cows graze and moo for their young when they wander out of sight. An innate mechanism brings cow and calf together as mealtime approaches. When it storms they run for the barn. When it's hot they find shade. When thirsty they meander to the pond. In the fall the calves are taken from their mother. They're ready to survive on their own, whatever their fate. The mother cows circle the fence around our house for days, each bawling for her baby. They're sure we humans inside the fence have something to do with their offspring's disappearance. You can probably put together many of your own analogies from here. But consider this: If your enemy, whatever it is . . . emotional disturbance, financial ruin, bickering family, abuse, wrong political agendas . . . were inside the fence, what would you do to take back what was yours? Would you brave the chasm under the piped cattle guard and leap for the life of your loved ones? Would you chance the abrasions of an all out charge against the rails of the fence? What about the electric fence that's there as a safeguard against you? . . . Its voltage could shock and burn. And what if the unimaginable took place? What if you stormed the gates of hell and lost your life?

How far are you going for the Lord? What price will you pay to be free . . . really free in your spirit? Are you waiting for someone else to rescue you? I dare say, they're not coming . . . It's just you and the Lord.

Concerning our nation, the Bible says, "Now the Lord is the spirit, and where the Spirit of the Lord is, there is freedom" (II Cor. 3:17). Every morning I rattle the gates, interceding in prayer for our country, its leaders, preachers, teachers, farmers, parents, children, etc., asking the Spirit of the Lord to dwell with us, and keep us in His ways and deliver us from the spirit of abuse and apathy, so we will remain free indeed.

In prayer, nervous and fearful of the future, I was asking God to help my family and me as we stumble through the tightrope act of politics. A family act, yes, but one which I alone must choreograph. He checked my spirit, revealing how I was asking amiss. I then chose to believe, rather than beg, as I prayed: "Thank You Jesus for helping us walk boldly, with our heads held high, standing tall and brave upon the path which You have placed us, and in the direction You have pointed us. Thank You for calling me to politics and allowing me to affect your world. Thank You that You will help me do it to Your glory."

God says, "Don't worry, watch and wait with willingness." He's such a cool God!

Why do people complain about politicians, yet seldom grumble about the rhetoric, lies, deception, and crooked ambitions of Satan? "For our struggle is not against flesh and blood, but against the rulers, against the authorities, against the powers of this dark world and against the spiritual forces of evil in the heavenly realms" (Eph. 6:12). I'm concerned that the energy we exert upon protesting poor leadership is a strategy from Hell to distract us from that which is effectual and pleasing to God. The Bible says we weary God with our words (see Mal. 2:17).

During a parent/teacher conference, I lavished praise upon the child of the family before me. Their daughter was an intelligent and intuitive little girl, and most likely, she will do well in life. I threw my arms open to accentuate my remarks, "Sarah is doing wonderfully in her work! She might just be our first woman president!" The father groaned and mumbled, "Oh, I hope she does better than that!" My heart sinks at such slurs.

I try to instill in my young students the sacrifice, privilege, and priceless worth of our country's freedom. We cite the Pledge of Allegiance each morning. Can you remember it? "I pledge allegiance to the flag of the United States of America and to the Republic for which it stands, one nation, under God, indivisible, with liberty and justice for all." One morning after our dry, recitation, I tried to jazz up the moment. "Free" happened to be one of our spelling words that week, so I jumped atop a student's desk, threw a declarative, victory hand high into the air and shouted, "I am so glad we are . . . ," then jumped down, ran to the wall chart and retrieved the flash card with the printed word "free." I held it up high in the air, thus cueing the students to complete my sentence, which most of them promptly did. As the others came alive, the most precocious of my little boys, quipped in his baby-talk voice . . . "We'ire not free; we'ire in school, Mrs. Morris!"

The following is a poem my sister wrote after visiting my family and me, on our ranch in western Kansas.

Dear little coyote, sing me a song
    Make it last the whole night long.
Golden sunrise bid me good 'morn,
    Do me well, sunflowers, wheat, and corn.

Great Plains embrace me, if you will,
    Just as if you were a Kentucky hill.
And if I should look back a bit forlorn,
    Help me look forward to a new hope born.

Oh Kansas, Oh Kansas, I am a pioneer,
    As those before me, sometimes I fear.
Can you accept me as your own?
    Here I stand, this is my home.

I'll give you all that is mine to give,
    To help you grow, love, and live.
And someday I know the Lord will bless,
    That you'll give back to me your very best.

—Cindy Hillard, Columbus, Ohio

Chapter Thirty-Three

If you have trouble forgiving me . . . or someone else . . . or yourself, then I implore you to embark upon an in-depth study of God's grace and mercy. Grace is an exquisitely beautiful treasure that God hands over freely to all those who ask.

Practice this quick prayer so it will be on the edge of your lips when needed . . . "Have mercy, Lord." Repeat it over and over until you can see, hear, smell, touch, and taste it. I breathe that prayer right now as I brace for the aftermath of the reading of this book. Some will despise me and cast me out . . . "Have mercy, Lord." . . . Some can't understand, though they want to . . . "Have mercy, Lord." Satan may create ways to deject me that I haven't considered. For those through which he works . . . "Have mercy, Lord." And as for me, while I remain firm in the anguish of writing these words for all to judge as they choose . . . "Have mercy, Lord." To you in the middle of tragic situations such as these *and far worse* . . . "Have mercy, Lord."

Resource Guide

If you find you need assistance with any area of your life, let me *first* suggest finding a church that is willing and able to help you. Pastors/congregations are not typically trained to handle detailed counseling but are usually open to providing a safe and supportive environment in which you can slowly find all your needs. Remember the task is the Lord's and yours. You mustn't blame others if you happen upon someone's lack of compassion, understanding, or indifference, that will only deepen your pain.

The *next* step is to read, read, read the Bible, along with tapping into the mammoth collection of books available on specific subjects just for you!

Then, your local courthouse can provide the phone numbers of agencies established to assist those in need. Many communities have local organizations already established that would be thrilled to reach out to you with informational materials and a listening ear. And of course, there's also 911.

Sometimes it's easier to heal by remaining anonymous, especially if you live in a small town. It's unfortunate, but for some reason we all want to believe the neighbor next door is perfectly stable and without heartache. I've included here a snapshot list of government/private organizations that can render secure and professional advice, without personal contact or disclosure.

Be Well, in Jesus' Name

Children/Teenagers

Youth Crisis Center Helpline
(24 hr) 800-332-6378

Child Find of America, Inc.
914-255-1848
800-I-AM-LOST
800-A-WAY-OUT

National Child Abuse Hotline, Child Help USA
(24 hr) 800-4-A-CHILD

National Children's Advocacy Center
256-533-5437

National Child Abuse and Neglect Clearinghouse
800-394-3366

National Association for Children of Alcoholics
714-499-3889

National Committee to Prevent Child Abuse
312-663-3520

National Referral Network for Kids in Crisis
800-KID-SAFE

National Center for Prevention and Treatment of Child Abuse
800-843-5678

Parenting

National Federation of Parents for Drug-Free Youth
417-836-3709

National Parents Resource Institute for Drug Education (PRIDE)
404-651-2548

National Families in Action
404-934-6364

Focus on the Family
800-A-FAMILY
www.family.org

Fathers' Resource Center
612-874-1509
www.slowlane.com/frc/

Parent Helpline
800-332-6378
www.KCSL.org

Parents Anonymous
800-421-0353

Media Concerns

American Decency Association
231-924-4050
www.AmericanDecency.org

Parents TeLewission Council
213-629-9255
www.parentstv.org

American Family Association
601-844-5036
www.afa.net

Morality in Media
212-870-3222
www.netcom.net/~mimnyc

Forum for Family Friendly Programming
www.ana.net/family

Federal Communications Commission (FCC)
complaints-enf@fcc.gov

Pregnancy

A Better Choice (Pregnancy Crisis Center)
316-612-2861

Pregnancy Counseling
800-848-LOVE

Hope Renewed (Pregnancy Crisis Center of Wichita, KS, Inc.)
316-945-9400

Fathers and Brothers Ministries
303-494-3282

MARC (Men's Abortive ReCovery) Ministries
610-384-3210

Marriages

Marriage Ministries International
303-933-3331
e-mail MMI@marriage.org

Crime Prevention

National Crime Prevention Council
202-466-6272

Criminal Justice

Juvenile Justice Clearinghouse/NCJRS
800-638-8736

Bureau of Justice Statistics Clearinghouse/NCJRS
800-732-3277

National Institute of Justice Clearinghouse/NCJRS
800-851-3420

Office for Victims of Crime Resource Center/NCJRS
800-627-6872

Domestic Violence

Battered Women's Justice Project
800-903-0111

Family Violence Prevention Fund/Health Resource
Center on Domestic Violence
888-792-2873

National Coalition Against Domestic Violence
303-839-1852

National Domestic Violence hotline
(24 hr) 800-799-SAFE
(TDD) 800-787-3224

National Network to End Domestic Violence
202-543-5566

National Resource Center on Domestic Violence
800-537-2238

Resource Center on Domestic Violence,
Child Protection and Custody
800-527-3223

Drugs/Alcohol

Adult Children of Alcoholics (AcoA)
213-534-1815

National Prevention Network
202-783-6868

Women for Sobriety
215-536-8026

Quest International
614-587-2800

Al-Anon Family Groups
212-302-7240

Alcoholics Anonymous (AA)
212-683-3900

American Council for Drug Education
301-294-0600

The Chemical People/WQED
412-622-1491

Coalition of Hispanic Health and Human Services Organizations
202-371-2100

National Clearinghouse for Alcohol and Drug Information
800-729-6686

Cocaine Anonymous
800-347-8998

CoAnon Family Groups
213-859-2206

Families Anonymous, Inc.
818-989-7841

Institute on Black Chemical Abuse
612-871-7878

National Mothers Against Drunk Driving (MADD)
800-438-6233

Nar-Anon Family Groups
213-547-5800

Narcotics Anonymous
818-780-3951

National Asian Pacific American Families Against Drug Abuse
301-530-0945

National Black Alcoholism Council
202-296-2696

RID-USA (Remove Intoxicated Drivers)
518-393-4357

Elderly

Older Women's League
202-783-6686

Administration on Aging/U.S. Dept. of Health and Human Services
202-401-4541

American Association of Retired Persons
202-434-2277

National Center on Elder Abuse
202-682-0100

National Committee for the Prevention of Elder Abuse,
Institute on Aging
508-793-6166

National Council on Aging
202-479-1200

Homosexuality

Unchained Love/Michigan Family Forum
800-644-9111
www.mfforum.com

Hate Violence

Center for Democratic Renewal
404-221-0025

Southern Poverty Law Center
334-264-0286

Missing Persons

National Center for Missing & Exploited Children
(24 hr) 800-843-5678

National Runaway Switchboard
(24 hr) 800-621-4000

Self-Help

National Self-Help Clearinghouse
800-621-4000

National Center for Prevention and **Treatment** of Child Abuse
800-843-5678

Sexual Assault

Center for the Prevention of Sexual and Domestic Violence
206-634-1903

Pennsylvania Coalition Against Sexual Assault
717-728-9740

Rape, Abuse and Incest National Network (RAIN)
(24 hr) 800-656-HOPE

The Kansas Community Access Network-Crisis Hotline
(24 hr) 800-END-ABUSE
www.ukans.edu/can

Support for Families of Homicide Victims

The Compassionate Friends, Inc.
630-990-0010

Parents of Murdered Children and Other
Survivors of Homicide Victims
(24 hr) 513-721-5683

Victims' Rights Information

National Organization for Victim Assistance (NOVA)
(24 hr) 202-232-6682

National Organization for Victim Assistance (NOVA)
(Information/referral) 800-TRY-NOVA

National Victim Center
703-276-2880
(Information/referral) 800-FYI-CALL

Office of Crime Victims Advocacy
800-822-1067

Victims' Assistance Legal Organization (VALOR)
703-748-0811

Political Issues

Call your local courthouse for ways to
Contact your Representatives, Senators, Governor, etc.

Concerned Women for America
202-488-7000
www.cwfa.org

The John Birch Society
920-749-3780

Center for Reclaiming America
877-SALTUSA
reclaimamerica.org

Freedom Under Fire
The Rutherford Institute
804-978-3888

The White House
1600 Pennsylvania Ave
Washington D.C.
202-456-7041